DEAR
YOUNGER
self

HOME

HOME

First Edition

Copyright © 2023 Kate Butler Books

www.katebutlerbooks.com

All rights reserved.

ISBN: 979-8-9881540-0-6

Design by Melissa Williams Design
mwbookdesign.com

This book is dedicated to you. We see you, we feel you, we relate to you, and we connect with you . . . because we are you. At our core, we are more alike than we are different. We are beings of light and love who deeply desire to make a positive influence on the world with our unique type of brilliance. The pages of this book promise to fill you with the wisdom, insights, and inspiration that will align you further with your soul's path. Our hope is that the vulnerability and authenticity of these pages will remind you deeply of who you are and inspire you to claim your dreams, shine your light, and step into the legacy you are meant to leave in this world.

It is your time. It is our time. It is time.

Enjoy the unfolding . . .

table of contents

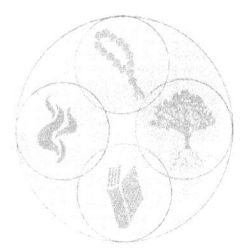

INTRODUCTION

A NOTE FROM THE CREATOR OF THE
INSPIRED IMPACT BOOK SERIES

Kate Butler, CPSC

This is to me, this is to you, this is to our dear, sweet, younger self . . .

Dear Younger Self,

It's simple, really, what I would whisper into the ear of my younger self . . . here goes,

My sweet girl,
You are strong.
You are capable.
You are enough.
You are worthy.
You can do hard things.
Things that may seem impossible also get to be easy, if you choose.

Love who you are and get there faster. The friction in life comes from the space in between loving yourself fully and feeling your deepest insecurity, which is that you're not good enough. When you are in this "in-between space," you are hurting—yourself and others. When you are in this space, you are questioning—yourself and others. When you are in this space, you are

1

judging—yourself and others. The only way out of this space is to fully love, accept, and appreciate yourself for all of who you are and what you are here to do.

My sweet girl, if I could tell you anything, I would tell you, get there faster.

It's not that life would look so much different, but it would *feel* different. You would probably choose the same paths, but you would save so many relationships, so many hearts, so many moments along the way. The sooner you get there, the richer life gets. The sooner you get there, the deeper you can go into your purpose and how you show up for others. The path may not change, but the impact does. Get there faster. Love yourself deeply. All of yourself. Accept your uniqueness and how you are different from others. This is what makes you shine, not what weighs you down. Appreciate yourself and that you choose to come here, right now, to this time and space, with this particular family, with this particular purpose on your heart and this life's soul mission to complete. Get there faster so you can do the work you came to do.

Get there faster.

You are worth it.

Your work is waiting.

You are loved beyond measure.

xo

With a Grateful Heart
— Kate ♡

ABOUT KATE BUTLER, CPSC

Kate Butler is a #1 International Best-selling and Award-winning author and speaker. As a CPSC, Certified Professional Success Coach, she offers clients dynamic programs to help them reach their ultimate potential and live out their dreams. She does this through Mindset, Success, and Book Publishing Programs. Kate is also the creator of the Inspired Impact Book Series, which this book is a part of.

Kate offers a variety of ways for her clients to share their inspiring stories with the masses, some of which are her live annual events, her Inspired Impact Magazine and Kate's TV show, *Where All Things Are Possible.*

Kate received her degree in Mass Communications and Interpersonal Communication Studies from Towson University in Maryland. After ten years in the corporate world, Kate decided it was time to fulfill her true passion and she began her journey of entrepreneurship. Kate also studied business at Wharton School of Business at The University of Pennsylvania and received her certificate in Entrepreneur Acceleration.

Kate now brings her expertise to mainstream media where she has been featured as the Mindset and Publishing expert on *Fox 29, Good Day Philadelphia, HBO,* in *The Huffington Post,* and on various other television, news, and radio platforms.

To learn more about becoming an author in the Inspired Impact Book Series, or to learn how to work with Kate directly on achieving your goals or publishing your book (including children's books), visit her website at www.katebutlerbooks.com. **To become an author in Kate's next book, visit www.katebutlerbooks.com.**

YES! We want YOUR story!

To connect with Kate

Facebook: @katebutlerbooks   **Instagram:** @katebutlerbooks
Website: www.katebutlerbooks.com

CHOOSE YOUR OWN ADVENTURE

Kim Demetreu

"**W**ho are you?" the psychic asked as she looked at me deeply with her intense, blue eyes. "Do you know who you are?" That was an unexpected response when I asked her about life after my upcoming (second) divorce. Surprisingly, I had no answers . . . and the adventure began . . .

* * *

Growing up as an only child, my favorite pastime was reading. My absolute favorite series of books was called "Choose Your Own Adventure." Every few pages, the story built up to a point where the main character needed to make a choice of what action to take next. For example: "When playing one day in the woods, Janey discovers a dragon. Would she run away through the forest? Turn to page 12. Or would she wake the sleeping beast? Turn to page 36." It was so much fun to reread the same book multiple times, making different choices at each turn to see all the variations of stories one book could bring you. It was like having over one hundred adventures in my hand at any given moment. Like many children, I didn't feel that I had a lot of choices in my life, so this book was pure magic to me.

The question from the psychic reminded me of a little girl who truly had no idea who she was and never felt she had any choices. Some would say her life resembled a dumpster fire. When she was eight years old, she was ripped from her happy little home near her family and friends to live a gypsy lifestyle. Her mom married her stepdad and changed her name (for a third time), and they moved every three months or so. They moved from one smalltown trailer park to the next, from one side of the country to the other. She had to get used to making friends and then losing them with each move for her stepdad's jobs. This was long before home computers and cell phones existed, when long-distance calls were simply too expensive unless it was an emergency.

They were a family of survivors, living paycheck to paycheck, and her parents were too busy working to teach the little girl all those things parents are "supposed" to teach little girls about becoming a woman. What made things worse was that she was very tall and awkward and had a woman's body at eleven years old. She was expected to act like, and was treated like, she was much older than the child she should have been allowed to be.

Some of those moves were great . . . new friends, new families, new schools, new adventures. And some were not so great as she learned that not everyone is very nice. Especially when certain people told her she was smart and pretty, followed by very uncomfortable touching in some very private places. She didn't enjoy the adventures that were often chosen for her, and she became rebellious.

She started working when she was eleven so she could buy her school clothes and have a birthday party that her parents felt they could not afford. (Make-at-home pizza and a sleepover was too expensive for them.) She did odd jobs around the community, picking up garbage after football games, picking peas from the field by the bushel, scooping ice cream at the local mini-mart, stuffing newspaper inserts, and she was even paid to clean one of her abuser's houses in her bikini (at twelve years old!). She didn't understand the intent that was behind that task at the time, but she was a survivor and did what she was told by her elders as she continued to try to be like "normal" kids on the outside.

She finally felt she was saved when her parents split and she moved back "home." However, she soon realized she no longer felt like she belonged there. Her friends and family had moved on and no longer had room in their lives for her. She continued to do what she was told to do, what was expected of her, and became what she thought she was supposed to be. She did well in school, made friends, fell in love (a lot), and became a single parent at twenty-one years of age. And so, her life of surviving continued.

Fast-forward twenty years, and she's living what was supposed to be her dream life, according to what she was told. She was in a middle-class midwestern suburban home with a husband, a son, a wooden picket fence, and her two and a half dogs for eighteen years. Her husband would eventually become more of a roommate, and they started living separate lives. She was a good mom, or at least she tried her best to be. Her goal was to prevent her son from experiencing the instability and abuses she'd experienced as a child.

She was a hard worker, working harder and longer hours than most of her peers but for a lot less money. Every year, she was rated as one of the best employees, but her peers were the ones getting the promotions and pay raises. It took her fifteen years to figure out how to excel in her career, and once she decided to stop being a worker bee, and become a Queen Bee, her career soared! She found mentors and asked for their advice and began reading and learning everything she could about the topics they recommended. The surprising thing for her was that it wasn't learning more about her day-to-day work that became the key to her success; it was developing her interpersonal and communication skills.

On paper, she had everything she thought—everything she was told—she wanted. She was *supposed* to be happy. She *should* have been happy. But all she felt was numb, like a robot that had been programmed to feel happy. Until one day, she became the one thing that she hated most in life: a hypocrite that shattered all her morals, beliefs, and values. It turns out she found her key to feeling happiness, to feeling alive in her heart and her soul, by breaking the morals and values that she'd been taught all her life and becoming the thing she hated most in this world.

Refusing to hate herself for finally feeling happy, she sought the advice and wisdom of her peers, mentors, and professionals to understand how her feelings and actions led her to this place of transition, including professional counseling and going to a psychic. Fast-forward to today, and she is blissfully living with her heart full of love, joy, abundance, and happiness in paradise with her soulmate! How did that happen? And how can you get there faster and easier than she did? How can you choose your own adventure?

Well, she, who you probably figured out is me, looked into a mirror, and I asked myself that same question the psychic did that day. "Who am I?" which was quickly followed up with "Who do I want to be?" And there, my dear younger self, is where your journey begins. How can you find your bliss? I wish I had all the answers for you, but let me tell you three key steps that worked for me.

1. Figure out who YOU are.

2. Decide who you WANT to BE.

3. CHOOSE to be that person and live your own adventure.

Wait, what? That's right, it seems too easy to be true, but that final one is the key. You have to make that choice once you figure out what happiness and success look like for you, on your terms. By learning that, you have a choice on how you think will determine what kind of life you live. That sounds crazy, but no matter what age you are, or what you've been through, you have the power to change your now *and* your future, but you must decide to choose. If you don't make choices for yourself, give yourself guidelines or a framework or a dream to work toward; there are plenty of people around that will be happy to put you to work for their purposes.

Let's break it down.

Step 1: Figure out who YOU are.

First, figuring out who you are . . . what does that mean?

Take a moment now, go to a mirror, look deeply into your own eyes, and ask yourself that very question. Who are you? Do you know? Do you love what you see? Don't look at the superficial exterior of you—your hair, your clothes, your accessories. Look . . . into . . . your . . . eyes. *Who are you*? Who do you *want* to be? Are you blissfully grateful to be living your life? Do you want to be?

Do you think you'll ever be what you *most* want to be? Do you even know what that is? Have you taken the time to think about it? I mean, really think about it! Not what your friends, families, or teachers have told you that you *should* be. Are you truly happy? What makes your heart feel light and makes you want to sing or dance spontaneously? Do you know what you want to do, how you want to live, and how you want to be treated?

If you are one of the 6–10 percent of the population that is actually living your childhood dream and you know without a doubt who you are, that's great! If you don't, don't worry, most of us were in that bucket at one point or another, and that's fine too. Each of us is on our own journey, and we're all trying to figure that out . . . until we do (then we often help others find their way too).

Figuring yourself out can mean a lot of things to a lot of people, but for me, it started with learning to be a better communicator. Which led me to learning about my communication and learning styles so I could better communicate with others and how to interact with their styles. From there, it snowballed into understanding love languages, values, priorities, strengths, likes/dislikes, goals, personality styles, and defining my vision of a "perfect" life? Whoa, that seems like a lot. It's not as overwhelming as it sounds once you get started. There are many tools out there to help you that have different focuses on personal and professional attributes, depending on what you decide you want to focus on the most.

Another very interesting and perhaps the most eye-opening exercise is to ask people what they think of you. They are often happy to tell you, and you may be pleasantly surprised to find out how others see you, instead of that less-than-perfect version that some of us see in the mirror. There are several ways to do this, but a very simple start is to choose three to five people and ask them for three words they would use to describe you. You may be pleasantly surprised to see or hear what you get back.

This type of self-exploration was the key to my career skyrocketing. It wasn't learning more about the technology that I worked on, as I'd presumed. It was literally learning how to be a better communicator and carefully defining my work persona based on the way I wanted my peers and executives to see me.

You may have thought that you are just born the way you are, communication styles, personality, and all; however, your communication style can be flexible, and your personality is simply a combination of how you think, how you act, and how you feel. The majority of those things are learned, including any insecurity, self-doubt, or perceived weaknesses, and you can unlearn and relearn yourself to a new personality and communication style to create your ideal persona.

Start paying attention to what you're thinking about, what you're focusing on, and what you're feeling. If you're feeling bad, ask yourself why and decide to change that thing you are feeling bad about. Pay special attention to the things you use to avoid boredom. We're often training ourselves to be drama magnets without realizing it due to what we're consuming through professional and social media. Those are the things that will shape our persona if we don't pay attention.

Just remember that you don't have to be everything to everybody. You get to choose who you want to be, and the first step is to understand who you are, why you think and feel the way you do, and what makes you tick . . . up until now.

Step 2: Decide who you WANT to BE.

Have you ever stopped to think about what you *want* to do, who you *want* to be, and what you *want* to have in your life? Seriously, so many of us spend so much time surviving and reacting to things that come into our path instead of choosing what we want our lives to be like. Sure, we make that annual birthday wish, and have little fantasies here and there . . . but do you really sit down and think, plan, or dream about your future?

Not just the material things, but what kind of relationships do you want to have? How do you want people to treat you, and you them? How much free time do you want? What hobbies would you like to have? How would you like to give back to your community? What kind of experiences do you want to have?

Do you know what you want or what will make you feel successful? Try starting with the things that you know make you happy. Take out a piece of paper, or your journal if you have one, and write down twenty things that have made you happy in the past. What made you laugh, smile, or just feel light in your heart? Try it now . . . I'll wait.

How does that feel? It's okay if you couldn't think of all twenty in one sitting. It took me a few sitting sessions when I started. If you're one of the lucky ones that had more than twenty that showed up on your first try, that's awesome! Now that you've got your happy creative juices flowing, write down at least twenty things that you want to *be, do,* or *have.* Go ahead, be silly and dream big!

For example, I love traveling, meditating on the beach, teaching, and spending time with my soulmate. Based on these things,

I'd like to have a part-time job with unlimited time off, where I get to teach people to become the best version of themselves, for *very* large amounts of money. Be specific when writing these things down. They will eventually turn into your goals you will celebrate someday, and it's a lot easier to work toward a "$200,000 salary" and a "month-long vacation in Thailand" than earning "a lot of money" and "traveling." How do you measure "a lot" and celebrate it when it comes true? (Traveling could just be to the grocery store in the next town over, so be specific!)

Once you figure out what makes you happy, you have the start of a plan. I recommend putting those things that you want on a vision board (a blank canvas or posterboard with pictures and words that display things that you want), and then create goals to add those things into your life to bring you more joy. You'll be amazed at how many of the things you put on a vision board will come true!

Step 3: CHOOSE to be that person and live your own adventure.

And that gets us to choice and choosing our own adventure. Regardless of where you live, what you believe, or what you are, one thing we have in common as humans is choice. You can choose what to focus your thoughts, time, and attention on. You can choose how to respond to any event in your life, positively or negatively. You can choose to learn what you want to learn, and you can choose what you think about. Thinking about your choices is how you can choose your life, instead of standing on the sidelines, waiting for what is given to you by others. Sometimes it's as easy as figuring out what you *don't* want and taking steps in your life to remove those things from your life.

It's also important to choose how you think about your circumstances. For example, did the little girl at the beginning of the story live a life of lack, loss, and abuse? Or did she get the opportunity to learn to live on pennies a day, constantly meet new people, and learn what type of people to avoid in her future? I was that little girl, and people always ask how I survived without the stability of a safe home, extended family, and consistent friends. I respond with the fact that I got to see new cultures, meet new people, and I learned a lot about what type of people I wouldn't allow my child to be around to keep him safe.

Just remember, you were born to be *you* . . . not a copy of someone else and not a regurgitator of everyone else's wants, beliefs, and desires. Only you can experience this world in the way you do, and only you have the combination of gifts and talents that are unique to this world. Think about it: no two people experience the same thing in the same way. Siblings or even twins that live in the same house with the same parents are two completely different life forces with different perspectives, personalities, strengths, values, filters, thoughts, preferences, and stories about their childhood.

You can't choose who you were born to, where you were born, where you were raised, or anything else from your past. However, you can change *how* you think about those things and how *often* you think about them. You can choose to live your life in the past, which can't be changed, or focus on the present and define your future. You *can* choose your own adventure; you just need to decide to make that choice.

* * *

PS: What would *you* do if you could become anyone you wanted to be for one year? For example, you were dropped into a foreign land, your past nonexistent, with your housing paid, money provided, and you can take one person that honors you like you are the sun and the moon? No past mistakes, no past judgments, no baggage, and nobody else's filters or perceptions to worry about.

Who would you become? What adventures would you choose?

Let me know, and I'll tell you what I chose in a year from now . . . And I'm off to my next adventure!

ABOUT KIM DEMETREU

Kim has been living adventures her entire life. Between thirty-seven moves, six last names, three marriages, and the treasure trove of family and friends that she gained and lost over time, she became a chameleon that could become who she "thought" she needed to be in order to provide value and to be loved and feel safe in her own home.

Once she decided to stop being a good little worker bee and become a Queen Bee in her career, she started on a self-development journey where she increased her corporate salary by $100,000, became an international technology speaker, became her own superhero, found her soulmate (who makes her feel like a beloved goddess every day), and is blissfully living her dream life on a beach in Hawai'i.

She left her twenty-five-year career in technology in 2021 to start a 501(c)(3) nonprofit, Inspirational Foundations, and a private training, coaching, and consulting company, KMD Executive Enterprises. Together they developed the Career Kickstart Bootcamp in order to help young women figure out who they are and who they want to be, teach them personal and professional skills, and introduce them to opportunities to get them there in a fun, casual, and supportive environment.

Her next adventure is taking her to a foreign land with her soulmate as they continue to find new ways to blissfully pursue their passions and inspire and empower women and children to become the best versions of themselves.

To connect with Kim

Email: kim@kmdexecs.com
Facebook: www.facebook.com/kim.demetreu
LinkedIn: www.linkedin.com/in/kimdemetreu/
Website: www.CareerKickstartBootcamp.com

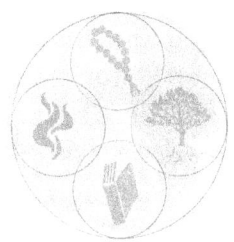

CREATING CLARITY THROUGH CHAOS

Angie Frontera

When was the first time you . . .
    Felt unworthy?
    Felt not good enough?
Felt not smart enough?
Felt like a waste of space?
Felt like a waste of oxygen?

When was the first time you felt like you weren't even sure you wanted to continue participating in life?

I was six years old, the oldest of what would eventually be five of us kids. I was living with my mom and biological father, Robert (a.k.a. sperm donor), and two younger siblings: a five-year-old sister and a few-months-old sister.

Long story short, Robert had friends over to the house to watch football. While all the adults were upstairs watching the football game, us kids were playing downstairs in the basement. While downstairs playing, one of the visiting kids used crayons and colored all over the inside of a book I checked out from the school library. It was the first book I had ever checked out. The teacher was very clear about how each of us was responsible for anything that happened to our books. I was terribly upset. I very quietly went upstairs to tell my mom what happened to my library book. I approached my mom's chair, crouched down on my knees to quietly whisper to her what had happened. Robert jumped up out of his recliner and headed for me. As kids, we knew better than to interrupt Robert's football games. Robert picked me up and literally threw me down a hallway, resulting in rug burns all over my face. Robert's friends gathered their kids and left. Of course, that was my fault too. And an excuse for Robert to start a fight with Mom, leave the house, and go to the bar to catch the rest of the game and get stupid drunk.

A week later when I returned to school, I was called to the school principal's office. The principal and two male police officers were waiting for me. I was told to strip down to my panties so they could check for marks and bruises. Being the compliant child I was, I did as I was told. I was mortified, embarrassed, and ashamed. I was silently crying. The tears were running down my face onto my flat, bare chest. I tried to be modest but was told to raise my arms up in the air and slowly turn. The principal and police were watching every move I made. No one seemed to care I was humiliated beyond measure . . . I wanted to completely disappear! All adults agreed I had no other bruises or marks and could get dressed again. I complied. I was sent back to class like nothing had happened.

But everything *had* happened for me.

I learned I didn't matter. My feelings didn't matter. My shame and embarrassment didn't matter. Other people and things (like football games) were more important than me. Whatever was said to me, whatever happened to me, I was expected to just "take it" and keep my mouth shut. People would not have my back or protect me. I was expected to cover for people to prevent them from getting into trouble. There was safety in keeping my mouth shut. When uncomfortable, just disappear. I learned when someone of authority tells me to do something, comply; do not ask questions, simply comply.

I learned to . . .
NOT defend myself,
NOT speak up for myself,
NOT take a stand for myself.

When I first learned about the opportunity to contribute a chapter to this book, I literally got chills from head to toe and broke down in tears! The title was *perfect*! I have told myself a million times over the last twenty-five-plus years something like, "I wish I had known that when I was younger so I wouldn't have had to figure so much of life out the hardest way possible."

When most of us are young, me included, we are absolutely positive we already know everything and don't need anybody, especially "old people" telling us anything. They're too old to understand anyway. I have told my adopted daughter so many times to listen with her heart, not just her ears, to what certain others have to say, learn from their wisdom and mistakes. I also know when we're young we think we're the exception and we're invincible!

Don't be like that! I've learned to listen to and learn from others' experiences—even when they're younger than I am. I believe we must always be open to learn from others' experiences, especially their hard life lessons. It could save us from some really dumb decisions and some real hard times down the road.

Never think something doesn't apply to you. Because it just might one day.

Never think something won't happen to you. Because it just might one day.

You are special, but not so special life won't hunt you down, tackle you to the dirt, chew you up, and spit you out. Life has a way of teaching some hard and fast lessons that will bring you to your knees and all but physically kill you.

There might even be times where life is so upside down, sideways, and every which way, that you will wish you were dead.

I did. In early 2014, I lost everything: my twenty-two-year-old very successful business and eventually our home due to over $180K being embezzled by my office staff in late 2010 during a very short time frame while my now ex-husband was in the hospital and rehab. Things got so horrible, the only thing that saved me from taking my own life was my adopted daughter, Ally.

Ally was almost nine years old in April 2010 when she came to live with me and my now ex-husband. Two months after Ally came to live with us, my ex told me that she needed to "go back." I'm like, "Go back where? What?!" She isn't a shirt you return to the store! It was at that point I gave him an ultimatum to live up to the promises he made to both of us or pack and leave. That felt really good! Liberating! I felt like I could breathe for the first time in years! I had been putting up with his refusal to help financially support our family and the emotional abuse for years. It was time. Finally in July 2012, he moved out.

I believe if Ally weren't with me in 2014, I'd be dead now. I was at that point, a single mom, working thirty-one hours a day, nine days a week. But if I offed myself, who would raise her? Who would love her like I did? Who would take care of her? Who would teach her what she needed to know to grow up? Who would take her to therapy? Who would be her advocate if I weren't here? After the honeymoon period with Ally, most of the time she wasn't the easiest. Being abused herself before she came to live with me, she brought plenty of her own emotional baggage to the party. We've been through some downright tough stuff over the years, for sure! I knew in Ally's heart and mind I was all she had. I didn't want to destroy her life again by taking mine. I would just have to figure a way through all that was happening in that temporary period of my life and get on the other side of it. And I did.

Today, I credit everything I've ever been through in my life with who I am today. I've been able to discover my true purpose in life on this side of paradise because of all the turmoil and craziness.

If it weren't for the decision to love and take on a foster child, I don't believe I would have ever gone down the road I did of learning about abuse, mental illness, what makes us tick, etc., and eventually become a coach.

I would have never learned what it was like to be a foster child at eight years old, to figure out a way to maneuver through the responsibilities of being a foster parent to a child who had been hurt and lied to by authority figures. I would have never felt at the core of my soul the shame that happened when I went from having a comfortable financial life to living on food stamps and scrounging around the house looking for change for gas money. The absolute worst part was when I had to "borrow" from the savings account I had set up for her. The agonizing fear, frustration, and drama of having strangers renting the downstairs bedrooms so we could stay in our home.

For most of my life, I was so busy trying to make everyone happy. It never occurred to me that I deserved to be happy. I honestly didn't know until a few years ago that I couldn't *make* anyone happy. All emotions come from within, even happiness. We can each only make ourselves happy. Nobody can ever make you feel a certain way. And when you "allow" yourself to feel emotions based on what others say or do, you are giving all your power to them. Despite what life is handing us at any given moment, we can still experience all the emotions, including joy and happiness.

I'll say it again: We cannot make someone feel a certain way!

You teach people how to treat you by what you allow. So how do you want to be treated? With love, kindness, respect, and understanding? Then demand that. Accept nothing less than that.

Why do we go through life and undermine our feelings? Why do we make excuses for people's behavior toward us (and others) and write it off as if we have done something to deserve their hateful, selfish treatment? Why do we feel we don't deserve better? Why do we feel so unworthy of great things? Why do we feel like literally everyone except ourselves is deserving of whatever they want? Why are we forever putting ourselves on the back burner?

Really sit with those questions for a few minutes.

Really contemplate your thoughts and feelings to those questions.

Get emotional about those questions.

Why is our self-talk so berating? Would you allow someone to talk to you the way you talk to yourself? I certainly hope not! Why is it easier for so many of us to take a stand for others, even take to the streets in protest, for what we believe to be unjust and unfair treatment of people but seem so completely unable to stand up for our own damn selves? It's time each and every one of us take a stand for ourselves. Stop believing all the smack people are vomiting out of their mouths and keyboards, whether it be about you or the world in general. Decide what you believe and take a stand. Quit being so wishy-washy.

Why do you allow all this BS drama in your life?

Aren't you worthy of happiness, love, and joy?

Why are you worthy of the life you want?

If you even had a *twinge* of not feeling one thousand percent deserving of the life you truly want at your core, you must examine that immediately! Ask yourself some deep, soul-searching questions. And don't stop till you can come up with some genuine responses. And if you're not bawling your eyes out and feeling like hammered hell at the end of all that, you're just lying to yourself. You're just sugarcoating. Get to the meat of your stuff! Then, go find a great coach to help you examine where all those BS stories come from and rewrite your story!

Get out and meet new people. Create great, lifelong friendships based on honesty, love, and trust. We all need a confidant we can call 24/7/365 when we need support. We all need that trusted soul to jump our poop when we are headed down the wrong path. Someone to jab us in the chest with their finger and ask us, "What the hell are you thinking?" Someone to keep us from making really dumb decisions. Someone that will jerk us out of harm's way. Someone that can genuinely be happy for us.

Staying in an abusive relationship led to many years of soul-destroying verbal and emotional abuse aimed at me for my "inadequacies." One thing I still find funny is the millions of times I was told my clothes were too loud, my perfume was too loud, my jewelry was too loud, my mannerisms were too loud.

Okay. So what? That was someone else's opinion of me. Was his opinion of me even true? Not to me.

For years, I allowed people to fill my head with their opinions of me. Who cares what their opinion is? The only thing that really matters is my opinion of me. My own self-image: How do I see myself? What qualities do I bring to the table? Am I pleasing to God?

Back when I was miserable and hated my life and everything about it, I would think things happened *to* me. I never considered that some bad things happened *for* me. I was listening to a web training. It hit me like a ton of bricks. My thoughts went to the way I was still feeling about spending so many years in a loveless, tumultuous marriage and in the embezzlement. I was so angry and disappointed in myself. I actually hated myself for putting up with so much crap, not taking a stand for myself, for allowing myself to be treated so badly for so long, for wasting the best years of my life for nothing! And just as quickly, it hit me: it is what it is, and all of that helped get me where I was at that exact moment in time. I would not be learning all the things I had learned over the last few years to be able to help others live their best lives if I hadn't experienced what I did. I wouldn't be learning to coach and help others by giving them hope and teaching them how they could also get peace in their lives.

So today, when something less than desirable shows up in my world, I ponder how to use this to my advantage. What can I learn from this? How can I use this to help others? Then I get to show up differently. I get to create something powerful and empowering for myself and others.

I was brutally reminded of that *for*-me-and-not-*to*-me lesson just a few months ago, in August 2022. I was unexpectedly admitted to the hospital for three days. While there, I was diagnosed with high blood pressure, type 2 diabetes, two bulging brain aneurysms, and a brain tumor. It took a few weeks to really wrap my head around all that. Then I started feeling depressed. I felt like, "Well, here I am, finally getting my life together again and truly happy for the first time ever. I have some money in the bank and my own home, a new grandson I love more than life itself, and this happens!" I started to default back to my old habits and my old thought patterns. Thank goodness for my family, some fabulous true friends, and an incredible coach who really love me! They really helped jerk me back. Real quick.

I believe all of this dis-ease came from all the years of turmoil, fear, and anxiety and not living as my true, authentic self . . . just wandering through life with no purpose. It finally caught up with me. So now instead of being angry or depressed about it, I get to do everything I can to reverse the situation and get healthy again. The diagnosis reminded me why I'm here and what I'm supposed to be doing. Now I get to create something powerful in support of myself and others.

You alone get to decide how you are going to show up—all day, every day, every second of every day. Why not show up powerfully? It is literally your choice!

In the last couple years, especially since my diagnosis in August 2022, I've learned that I'm exactly where I'm supposed to be. I've come to love and value myself again and realize that I do deserve whatever I set my sights on. I'm running a successful business with my mom, I'm building my coaching business, helping raise my grandson, and volunteering. I get to learn about whatever I choose to on a daily basis.

After losing almost everything and basically starting over

from scratch, I have an entirely new perspective on what's most important to me. My dreams and goals have changed drastically from several years ago. I get to be my true authentic self and make decisions on what I want and what I feel is best for me and my family. I get to coach and mentor amazing people who also want to create the best life possible for themselves and their families.

I'm genuinely happy at my core for the first time in my life!

If I can do all that, you can too!

I hope I gave you some value today with some of my experiences and thoughts. If so, I'd love to hear from you.

If you are interested in the possibility of being coached and creating your own incredible possibilities, please feel free to reach out to me via email at Coaching@AngieFrontera.com. I'd love to create something powerful with you!

ABOUT ANGIE FRONTERA

Angie Frontera is a certified Transformational Life Coach who empowers women to be their authentic selves by helping them discover their own hopes and dreams so they, too, can leave a dent in this world. She utilizes several diverse tools to help her clients learn how to appreciate their unique value. Some of the tools she utilizes are EFT, NLP, meditation, Jack Canfield's Success Principles, and others. One of her goals is to love and help guide everyone she meets toward a powerful, peaceful life in harmony with God's purpose for them.

Angie strongly believes in the empowerment of life happening *for* you, not *to* you. She believes there is a lesson in almost everything, and what we do with that lesson will influence the quality of our lives for the great or not so great.

Angie is a mom, daughter, sister, aunt, and nonna (Italian for *grandmother*). She enjoys quality time with family and friends. Angie is one of four generations sharing a home in Pigeon Forge, TN, USA. She loves to travel both domestically and internationally. She absolutely loves and adores her new grandson born in December 2021. She loves teaching and playing with him while watching him change from a baby to a little boy as his personality develops into a young man.

To connect with Angie

www.AngieFrontera.com
Coaching@AngieFrontera.com
Facebook: AngieFrontera0412
Instagram: @AngieFrontera
LinkedIn: AngieFrontera

FROM SHELTER TO CEO

Kristy Whilden

Hey there, you beautiful human. I see you. Stop crying right now and pay attention. You don't know me yet, but you will. I know you feel hopeless, worthless, and inept. You have officially hit rock bottom. But what you don't know is something incredible has also just happened. The moment you decided to move to the rape and abuse shelter to protect your children and start your own healing journey, you were planted. And it is now time to grow. You have been hurt, neglected, and abused. Yet you are so strong. When that so-called dung heap of a "*man*" decided to drug your wine, take every ounce of dignity you had left, and toss it in the trash like the garbage he is, you know what you did? You survived. How do I know all of this? Because . . . #MeToo . . . I am you.

You have to suck it up and move forward. There are three little people counting on you.

Across the hall finally sleeping peacefully is your beautiful little girl. She is fighting battles you cannot see but you know are there. Trust your mommy gut. She needs you now more than ever. Hug her every day. I know you were young when you had her and had no idea what you were doing, but she forgives you.

She loves you something fierce because you are the only thing steady in her life. She is your inspiration, best friend, and your rock. Your daughter will graduate from college at eighteen on a life path inspired by you. What a beautiful gift you will receive the day she becomes your business partner.

Look in the bed next to you. That's your baby boy. He will be your savior through this difficult time. He may only be four years old now, but you will soon see how truly fantastic he is. When you are at your worst, hug him. His hugs move mountains. Sometimes he knows you need him before you do. Treasure every interaction with him. He's not only your savior but your daughter's as well. Because of you, he will become a LEGO-building, gifted and talented, Irish-dancing machine. He loves school and has many friends. He is a true gentleman. You have always been and will continue to be his number one.

Being a special needs mother is very difficult. But your other little guy down the hall will become your source of strength. Being there fighting his battles with him and not against him is the catalyst to forming the most perfect mother–son bond with him. I cannot wait for you to see how your son grows into this handsome, brilliant young man. His needs will catapult you into a better life with amazing opportunities and friendships (for you and him). I know you are fearful that he will never find a true friend. Well, he meets his best friend in middle school, and a beautiful cheerleader just asked him to her high school semi-formal. Yep, he's a stud. He now loves his high school, has straight As, and is studying nuclear energy. His teacher says he's the top of his class, and he is a sophomore in a class of seniors. You're doing everything right with him. One thing that I do ask is for you to keep him focused on playing the piano. He is talented beyond measure. Nurture that. He will teach you the true meaning of unconditional love. This boy will do anything for you.

Look at all you have accomplished so far. The moment you learned you were pregnant with your daughter, you enrolled in college. You went to CNA school and community college at the same time. You graduated with three associate degrees. You then put yourself through nursing school and were a psych nurse for fifteen years to a brain-injured client. Through a breakup, a car accident, and a diagnosis for your child, you stayed focused on your goal and finished your bachelor's degree. You created and opened a preschool and ran it for four years. Yes, you had to sell it, but the incredible women who bought it now have four. Your ideas are not garbage like you think they are. You just never had the right support backing you. After yet another breakup, you held onto your pride and joy with all of your might—your music school.

Do you remember how you felt looking up at your music students sitting at that beautiful Steinway piano on the stage of the prestigious Carnegie Hall in New York City? What an accomplishment that was. You were such a good teacher—no, you were and still are a *great* teacher. Your teacher was Liberace's protégé, remember? Your parents gave you only the best. Such a gift. You were on top of the world. But still you thought you were worthless. Little did you know there was something looming in the background that would change your life forever.

"I'm sorry, Miss Whilden, but you have moderate to severe progressive sensorineural hearing loss and will be deaf by the time you are forty-five." The words from the audiologist swirled in your mind as violently as your vertigo and screeched like your tinnitus as the doctor fit on your first pair of hearing aids. *This couldn't possibly be true.* You only noticed a short time before that your kids were complaining the music in your car was too loud. It was just last week that you realized you asked "What?" one too many times and people started answering with "Nevermind." You went home and sobbed . . . for days. Once again, you felt worthless. Who is Kristy Whilden without *music?* Music was your lifeline.

Left heartbroken thinking your teaching career was over, massive depression set in. *What now?* You do what you do best:

your love for learning sends you back to school. The first day of class, you meet a teacher of the Deaf who knows British and American Sign Language. She catapults you into the Deaf World through a whirlwind of information, videos, and panel interviews. She has a way of making you feel . . . well . . . normal. When the d/Deaf culture class was over, you wanted more, so you officially applied for the degree in American Sign Language and Deaf Studies. The ASL classes and teachers were so welcoming. But only one of these professors changed your life. He was and still is kind, cool, smart, very fun, and Deaf. You explained to him your hearing loss journey, and he took you under his wing. He suggested that your daughter come to class so she'll never lose communication with you. She was only thirteen then.

Remember the honors society induction for your daughter? Because you didn't register as deaf prior to the program, there were no seats close enough to the interpreter. You sat on the bleachers watching your daughter walk across the stage with tears streaming down your face because you couldn't even hear them say her name. It was a struggle to see the interpreter, and you were not sitting close enough to read the lips of the people on stage. Everyone sounded like they had marbles in their mouth. You really wished the interpreter was on stage where everyone could see them. This was a very difficult day but truly a pivotal moment. You had an idea.

You talked to your daughter, and she said exactly what you had been longing to hear. "Mom, you cannot lose your love of the performing arts forever. We can do this!" Together you decided to start a d/Deaf/hearing theater where the students are the actors and interpreters on stage. You both wanted to promote equality. You desperately wanted everyone's eyes (d/Deaf and hearing alike) to be off the interpreter in the corner and onto the stage to be able to enjoy the acting/dancing props/lighting. Hands Up Silent Theatre was founded to do just that. At Hands Up Silent Theatre, our mission is to encourage the d/Deaf to learn more about the performing arts and the hearing to learn American Sign Language and interact with d/Deaf peers. Together, we create performances for the d/Deaf and hearing to enjoy as one!

You were on top of the world again! Until your little Tinder date gone wrong. Now here we are, back in our room at the shelter. You are defeated, but in the end you will win. Everything is going to be okay. And this is where my story begins. I'll explain how you get from you now to me in the future. You will soon meet a man who is very kind to you. From him, you will gain back your creativity and confidence. Then there is someone you have already met that you do not realize will completely change your life for the better. Tomorrow you will have a nervous breakdown at your theater. She will sit next to you. Tell her everything. She is a safe person. Between these two angels, your life will be catapulted in a completely different direction. Are you ready? Let's go.

Within one week, you will have a brand-new job teaching ASL musical theater at a charter school and your own apartment. Your special needs son will also attend this middle school and find his very best friend. Your angels will help you move out of the shelter and into your new life. Everything is going just perfectly for a couple of years. Exciting, right? Cue a pandemic . . . COVID-19. You and your daughter catch COVID . . . twice . . . and survive. The boys somehow escape unscathed. During this unprecedented time, however, you were able to take a step back and focus on your family. With much consideration, you decide to shut down your music school for good. Through this sadness comes great redemption. You file the paperwork and Hands Up Silent Theatre gets approved to become a 501(c)(3) nonprofit! (Cue the fireworks!)

People believe in your mission. People believe in you! You are not a loser. You are not worthless. You now have a beautiful, blended family with three extra bonus kiddos in a gorgeous home of your own. You have a new job as an ASL and musical theater instructor at one of the most prestigious private high schools for girls in NJ. Hands Up is growing every year. Your children are all doing great! Your special needs son has straight As, *loves* high school, is studying nuclear energy, and is taking college classes at age fifteen. Your little guy trains with professional Irish dancers. Your daughter is your co-founder and COO of this beautiful company and plans to become a teacher of the Deaf. She is working toward her master's degree at age eighteen.

Your brother loves the heck outta you. He was your first very best friend. You now have three more best friends that will do anything for you. You *are* worthy of love. There was even a play written about you that was performed on the Stockton University Black Box Theater stage. You have taught well over five hundred students basic ASL. Some of those students have decided to dedicate their lives to the d/Deaf community by becoming interpreters and d/Deaf educators and are attending universities to do so. You have read ASL stories to your son's classes and local libraries. You have helped to start after-school ASL clubs. You and your students performed the national anthem at the Eagles stadium, local parades, and with the well-renowned Philadelphia Girls Choir. Not only that, but you and your students have performed ASL musical theater in front of thousands of people at some of the most beautiful theaters in southern NJ.

Yes, you are Kristy Whilden, lowercase D deaf, hard of hearing, late-deafened adult. But you are also Kristy Whilden, founder and CEO of Hands Up Silent Theatre, author, and mother of six! But wait! The best hasn't happened just yet. Remember your beautiful piano that you turned away from? Well, don't listen to your first audiologist. She was wrong. Yes, your ears are changing. But they will not (at least not for a long time) reach eighty decibels of hearing loss. Do you know what you can still hear now at age forty-one? A jet plane . . . and a piano. :)

So, where does life take me from here? I have gone back to school to earn a Master's in Fine Arts in Creative Writing (MFA). I want to spread my love of d/Deaf culture and representation from the theater world to the literature world. I also want to encourage authors to write characters of all abilities into their stories and screenplays. Becoming an international best-selling author sounds pretty great too. I recently found a doctorate degree program in Ireland for creative writing. Reach for the stars, right? I certainly will take my dream trip to tour Ireland and Scotland. I want to walk where my ancestors once did. From theater to books to the big screen, you never know where you might see me next.

To my dear thirtyish-year-old self, your story is one of resiliency. No matter what pushes you down, all you have to do is look into the eyes of your children and you have no choice but to stand back up. Not only that, you need to stay strong for the many students you get to inspire day after day. In order to be resilient, it is a necessity to find your purpose and allow it to be the fire inside of you to stand up and continue to move forward with your life. I wrote my story in hopes that it will get into the hands of the next girl sitting on a rape and abuse shelter bed wondering if she matters. You do matter. You are the star of your life. Shine bright.

ABOUT KRISTY WHILDEN

Kristy Whilden is a mother of six, teacher, entrepreneur, former nurse, and music educator with a BA from Rutgers University who owned a music school for over ten years. In 2014, Kristy was diagnosed with progressive sensorineural hearing loss. She went back to school and obtained a degree in Deaf Studies and American Sign Language from Rowan College at Burlington County.

At this time her focus turned from music to musical theater. She wanted all d/Deaf eyes on the stage and not always having to rely on the interpreter on the floor. Hands Up Silent Theatre nonprofit was created. With Kristy as founder and CEO and her daughter Hailey as co-founder and COO, they encourage the d/Deaf to learn more about the performing arts and encourage the hearing to learn ASL and interact with d/Deaf peers. Together, they create performances for the d/Deaf and hearing communities to enjoy as one!

Miss Whilden is now back in school getting her MFA in creative writing at Southern New Hampshire University. Although her life is d/Deaf theater, her real love is d/Deaf history and writing. As an aspiring author, published journalist, and playwright, Kristy is hoping to write novels with d/Deaf characters and representation of all abilities. It is also her goal to encourage everyone to learn ASL to help bridge communication gaps between the d/Deaf and hearing cultures and to promote inclusion and access in every aspect of life.

To connect with Kristy

handsup-theatre.org
kristywhilden@gmail.com

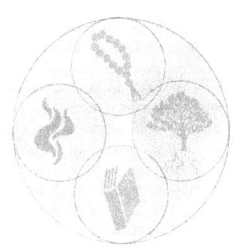

THIRTY-TWO

Amber Whitt

Hey, you. It's me, your forty-two-year-old self. I see you sitting in the car sobbing, and I know you just received some really scary news. Do you mind if I come sit in the passenger seat of the car with you? I know you are terrified. I know you have a five-month-old baby at home, and I know you're still breastfeeding. I know you've just lost your mother-in-law to Stage IV cancer. You've just celebrated your thirty-second birthday and your third wedding anniversary. I know you just went in for your mammogram and ultrasound and were told previously that the lump was "nothing to worry about, it's probably just a clogged milk duct." This is the first time you've been talked to about the serious potential of having breast cancer.

I want to sit here in this moment with you. I have some things to tell you, and I want to reassure you. I know how hard this is to wrap your head around, and this is just the beginning of this journey. Cancer at age thirty-two? It's heavy, I know. I remember it like it was yesterday. Everything you're about to go through is going to grow you in so many ways, and the best part is you're going to be okay. Take a deep breath and let me hug you for a minute. Let me just whisper softly into your ear . . . "You're going to be better than okay; you're going to come out on the other side of all of this not just surviving it but absolutely thriving. I love you; your resilience is what will get you through all of this."

When I was young, I never really wanted to get married, or have kids. I always envisioned myself living my best life, in a mansion, on top of a hill, with more rescue dogs than I could count. I wanted to be a successful business owner, in charge of myself, with a deep passion for rescuing dogs. Those visions and dreams changed when I met James, the love of my life. We got married on a private beach in Cabo San Lucas, Mexico, in September of 2009.

Shortly after we were married, I left the corporate world in search of finding what I truly wanted to do. I have always loved helping others and have gravitated toward that my entire life. If I wasn't helping humans, I would be helping all the stray animals. I've been an entrepreneur from a young age with my own dog-sitting and dog-walking business. After high school, I studied to become a licensed esthetician and had my business helping others to feel and look their best. I ventured into the medical side of the industry and grew with a corporate esthetics company very quickly. The promotions happened very fast. I was very highly requested by clients, and my sales figures were top notch. However, the corporate structure wasn't what I wanted. How could I create a business for myself that would fulfill me and help others? My passion for helping others led me down several interesting paths, but one really struck me.

After helping many busy families with their home cleaning needs and seeing how it impacted their lives, I decided to start my own small cleaning business. I giggle now thinking back on this new endeavor—just me and a vacuum, as James used to say. I saw how it relieved so much stress off people and gave them valuable time back with their family, and to them I was a godsend. Cleaning for me was and still is absolutely therapeutic. Clients were referring me to their friends and family, and I was busting my buns going to grocery stores and anywhere else I could to hang up signs. Social media wasn't a thing back then; word of mouth was the way to go. My personality, honesty, character, staying true to my word and following through, and what I brought to people's lives were king. I never anticipated having employees. Back then it was just going to be me: small, easy, and very lucrative. I was loving it. Hard work pays off, right?

The spring of 2011, some dear friends of ours welcomed their baby girl into the world, and we caught the fever—baby fever! We decided to try and have a baby of our own. I had been told by my doctors I wasn't able to have children and was uncertain how this would go for us. But sure enough, we happily announced in August of 2011 that we were having a baby girl, and we could not have been more thrilled and excited. Our dreams of starting our own family were coming true. Mackenzie Sophia was born May 1, 2012. She was perfect.

Within a couple of months, we asked her doctor about the flat side of her head and noticed she always had her head tilted to one side. She was diagnosed with torticollis, was prescribed physical therapy, and would need to get fitted for a helmet to help reshape her head. Our perfect baby would start physical therapy to strengthen her neck muscles and would be in a helmet for at least twelve hours a day for about six months. We were first-time parents and struggled with her being in a helmet, but physical therapy made her so strong. Long before she was supposed to roll over, crawl, stand, or walk, she was doing it, and she was months ahead of other babies her age physically. She was the epitome of strength.

It was shortly after Mackenzie's birth that my mother-in-law was diagnosed with Stage IV cancer. This came as a shock to all of us. She passed within a few months of her diagnosis, and this hit all of us hard. We knew she was no longer in pain and was now at peace, but the grief James and his siblings faced was hard.

Two weeks after her passing, we celebrated our third wedding anniversary and my thirty-second birthday. I went in for my annual lady exam and was excited to talk about my new venture of motherhood with my OB-GYN. She delivered Mackenzie, and I was preparing for an "all good, see you next year" kind of exam. When we got to the breast portion of the exam, she stopped quickly when she felt the lump in my right breast. She asked me how long it had been there and why I hadn't told anyone in the doctors' group about it. I let her know that when James and I came in for my four months checkup, there was a very small lump in my right breast. We mentioned it to the doctor in the group I was scheduled to see; he felt it and assured me it was nothing to worry about and that it was probably just a clogged milk duct. He said after I have my daughter and when I finish breastfeeding her, it would simply go away. We listened to him and trusted him.

It was my first pregnancy, my body was no longer just mine, things weren't normal any longer since I was growing a human, so hearing it was no big deal calmed any fears we had. My OB-GYN was not so calm and passive about this lump. It had grown significantly while I was pregnant, but I was still breastfeeding, and I really hadn't thought much else about it. She made some calls and asked me to go get a mammogram and ultrasound done ASAP to see about the lump. In my head, I was still thinking it was a clogged milk duct, but I would be happy to go to put her mind at ease.

With my breasts full of milk, I went in for my first mammogram followed by an ultrasound of my right breast. I was nervous, but I kept assuring myself that everything was fine. My nerves were high because I had never done this before. I remember the technician asking me why I had waited so long to come in for an exam. I told her what my doctor had said and that I was still breastfeeding my daughter. I really hadn't thought about it. Honestly, I was still adjusting to being a new mom, my sweet baby girl in a helmet and regular physical therapy, my mother-in-law just passing, and now I was being asked why I had waited. I trusted my doctor. Looking back now, I wish I had pushed harder and questioned more about what was happening to my breast and body.

When the doctor came in to review my ultrasound, he asked me harshly, "Why did you wait? The chances of this lump being cancer is very significant. You should have come in months ago." I was stunned. I couldn't even begin to think or process what he had just said, and then came the real deal. I would need a biopsy. He stood up, paused for a moment, and then looked me directly in the eyes and said, "There is a ninety-nine-percent chance this is cancer, and you're about to face some really hard decisions, and you'll need to listen to your team of doctors as they guide you and advise you on how to get through this." *Cancer.* I thought I was there to talk about a clogged milk duct. Talk about shock.

I sat in my car in the parking lot and sobbed. I could not even begin to wrap my head around this, let alone break this news to James, or my family. The biopsy came next, and then we waited. We were leaving the children's hospital downtown where Mackenzie had her helmet resized regularly. We were just about to hop on the highway, and my phone started ringing. It was the doctor who I had met with prior to my biopsy. She said she called me as soon as the results hit her desk, and she started off by apologizing to me. "I'm so sorry, Amber. You do in fact have breast cancer."

Those words hit me like a ton of bricks. I couldn't breathe, I couldn't think, I couldn't do anything except pass the news to James as he was driving and burst into tears. Why is this happening to me? What did I do wrong? The guilt and sadness I felt on that drive home was horrendous. We let all our family know the results.

The fear, shock, questions—it all came as a massive wave, as did the never-ending love and support. I decided to share my story and everything that was about to unfold on my social media. I thought, *Let's be real, let's be transparent, let's be honest, and let's make sure everyone knows that this can happen to anyone at any given time!* I was going to become an advocate. I was thirty-two years old, healthy, and breast cancer does not run in my family. Cancer knows no boundaries. It doesn't care your age, sex, ethnicity, social economic status; it doesn't care what else is already on your plate.

Next came a lot of visits with a lot of doctors, surgeons, oncologists, radiology, and the plans for how to overcome this. My mindset was one hundred percent positive. Not only was I ready to beat this, I was ready to kick the doors off the hinges, letting anyone and everyone know what I was going through. "Have you had your mammogram this year? If not, you should." That became my motto. "Self-exams save lives."

The outpouring of love and support was extraordinary! Friends, family, and even strangers were reaching out. Meals were delivered; care packages were dropped off and sent our way. Blankets, hats, and scarves were made for me. I was astonished by how many people were willing to help and support us. A friend made shirts with "Cancer Sucks" on them and gave us all the proceeds. We were beyond blessed to have such an amazing and compassionate support system. Along with that positive mindset came some anxiety and sleepless nights. How was I going to be a mom, a wife, a business owner, and juggle everything and get myself healthy again? I was going to push forward no matter what.

Real conversations were happening. As if the cancer diagnosis wasn't enough of a hit to us in year three of our marriage, we had to decide the future of our family. I remember a visit with my oncologist. She had asked me several times if I wanted to freeze my eggs to plan for our future. Because my cancer fed off my hormones, I would be on an estrogen blocker for ten years following my surgeries and finishing chemo and radiation treatments. I would be nearly forty-three with that timeline. I was struggling to make a real decision. We wanted more kids. She said to me, "Let's say you decide in ten years to get pregnant again, and you have a recurrence, and this time around you're not so lucky, and you don't survive it. That leaves James raising Mackenzie and a new baby by himself. Are you okay with that?" That stopped me in my tracks. No more babies for us. No siblings for Mackenzie. That was beyond hard to process, but the decision was made.

James was with me for every surgery and every chemo treatment. I lost all the hair on my body. No eyelashes! I didn't care about losing the hair on my head, but I sure did miss my eyelashes. When I finished my thirty-third ongoing daily radiation treatment, James was there to video me walking out of my final treatment, where all of my chemo nurses and oncology and radiology team were there waiting for me to *ring the bell!* Ringing the bell signified I was done with treatment. I went in for my final scan and received the call that we had been waiting and praying for: I was cancer-free!

We planned a luxurious, adults-only getaway to celebrate! I remember this conversation with James so vividly. We were in the pool, surrounded by palm trees and soaking up the hot Mexico sun. I was alive, I was motivated and determined, I wanted to come back home with a fierce fire under me, and I wanted to blow the business up massively. I came up with a plan to hire and train and make my small business/one-woman show into something much bigger. I told him exactly what I wanted to do and how I was going to get there.

Guess what? I made it happen. I manifested and created and worked very hard and diligently. I did not ever give up on myself or my dream. I did exactly what I set out to do. I created the life I had dreamed of.

I've had my company now for nearly thirteen years. I get to help families every day, and I get to employ people and help benefit their lives. The business gained so much success James was able to quit his job, and he now helps me run our business. I got my big house and my rescue dogs. I also got the two biggest blessings of my life: my husband James and my amazing Mackenzie Sophia.

Cancer is not a death sentence. I know that not everyone survives their cancer diagnosis. But I survived. I'm here for a reason. I am relentlessly thankful and full of gratitude that I get to be here every day to love my daughter unconditionally and see her grow up. I want you to know that there is hope, there is support, and there is always possibility! Your mindset is so important! I'm so graciously proud of myself for never giving up and having the courage to face this all head-on. I get to be a voice and an advocate, and I offer myself as a shoulder for anyone to lean on in their time of uncertainty. I've made a lot of amazing connections along this journey, and I love that people will reach out to me regarding their loved ones and how to overcome and how to support them. My biggest piece of advice is making sure they know they're loved and supported. Those conversations can be uncomfortable, but they're necessary.

To my younger self, I am so proud of you. Through your resilience and unwavering positive mindset, you have overcome so much, and through this journey, I have come to understand what matters most. Travel more, adventure more, help others, spend time with the ones you love. Tomorrow is not ever promised, and I'm so thankful to still be here on this Earth to offer you hope and the courage to keep going and keep pushing forward. You are powerful, you are capable, and sharing this story gives me strength, as I hope it helps you as well.

ABOUT AMBER WHITT

Amber is a wife and a mom, and she is a small-business owner. She has received several awards over the years for her excellence in business development, communication, marketing, strategizing, and sales. Amber is also a licensed esthetician and a certified Quantum Reiki energy healer. She enjoys helping others all over the world in many ways.

Amber is very passionate about animal rescue; she has two rescue dogs and has helped save countless animal lives over the years. Amber really loves the outdoors, hiking, kayaking, swimming, boating, floating down the river, and spending time with her family and friends. Amber loves to travel, read, and practice energy work! Amber is an advocate for breast cancer awareness and has made a lot of long-lasting relationships bonded by an incurable disease, cancer.

To connect with Amber

www.amberwhitt.com
amber@amberwhitt.com
Instagram: @awhitt0922
Facebook: Amber Whitt

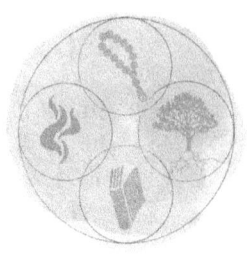

THE CHOSEN ONE

Jodie Baudek

You are a beautiful, unique human being. You aren't weird or different. The world is afraid of your confidence. No one understands your gifts, your insight, your intuition that serves you so well. You are strong and courageous. What you experience and share with the world will allow you to touch and change millions of people. You take ordinary moments and follow signs that make them become extraordinary opportunities. You don't worry about the hows, whys, or let fear get in the way. You let God take care of that, and you follow God's winks along the way. You are given the big picture and allow yourself to follow your heart. You allow the pieces of the puzzle placed in front of you to fall into place. You are open to seeing, accepting, and realizing your blessings. Shine on, and screw the jerks that try to dim your light. Walk through this world like you belong here: head held high with a smile on your face. Let others pick up on your uniqueness. Share your confidence—your gift.

Oftentimes, you are going to be given a really hard time when you are younger that you don't do your schoolwork the way people think you are supposed to do it. You do the end project and you work your way backward, and you always figure it out.

You are going to find in your thirties that you have something called dyslexia. It had never been diagnosed; you just knew you flip your numbers. You don't understand things, and your brain operates differently. Understand that dyslexia is not a disability, and don't take it, hinder it, or claim it is a disability or think that something is wrong with you, because people will have disabilities. There is nothing wrong with disabilities; you just have to learn differently and do things differently. That dyslexia is going to end up being a gift of yours because of your ability to let your brain flip around and be able to do things reversed.

You are going to have very many practical, normal moments in your life that turn into extraordinary moments for you. You see, my friend, there is one thing that is unique about you and you don't even know this: you just expect miracles to happen. When you see something, you see the love in it. Don't get me wrong, you know what you want, you have your ghetto side to you, you have your sassy side, and you will know you are the angel on your friend's shoulder, but you are also the devil on their shoulder too—all in fun.

You have a unique ability to attract beautiful opportunities. Here is how it works. You stay humble. That is the biggest thing that I want you to do. Stay humble but expect miracles. So when things are happening and people are asking you why they picked you, why this, why that, don't question and wonder why. Think to yourself, *Why not me?*

I'm going to give you a perfect example of something and you'll have no idea where it leads. You are going to be in your happy place, lying there, watching Oprah Winfrey, and you are very stressed because you don't have any idea how to keep making all these things happen in your life that you know you are destined to do. While watching *Oprah*, Kriss Carr, Gabby Bernstein, Marie Forleo, and Mastin Kipp were guests, and you knew you should be on *Oprah*. *How do I do that?* You practice your meditation. You lie down and remember you are going through something in your life. There is a storm going on around you, but you are not allowing it to be inside of you. As you are meditating, you ask, *How do I do this? How do I take myself through all of these things? I know that I have a higher calling than what I am doing now. Yes, I am making an impact during the storm, yet there is so much more.*

After you come out of meditation, you look to the side and there is the book: *The Secret.* You open the book because you always believe that when you ask a question, your answer will come. You open the book to the story, "Chicken Soup for the Soul."

You have an instinct to connect with friends who know celebrities in Los Angeles. Your friend tells you to start a Twitter account. You have no idea how to do social media. You are lucky if you can send an email at this point in your life. You open a Twitter account and (I want you to always remember that there are no accidents) somehow, someway, when you log in and check your account to make updates, you can't. You understand with social media your name is your name and if you can't get back into your account, you are going to lose your name. You calmly try to find out who this person is by sending them an email. You ask them if they can log into the account and figure out why they have your stuff. As you are doing this, you think, *Oh, I'll buy the domain name.*

One of your friends is doing some research for you and finds that this person has the domain name, which has the same name beginning as yours. The name of your business is Essence of Life. Your email says, "Hey, I was interested in writing a book, and for some reason, you have my email address. I don't know why. Could you please log in and give me permission to have my account back?" This person graciously says, "Yes, absolutely. By the way I am an editor." Oh! Okay. You end up having a beautiful conversation with this person, who is a beautiful soul and an editor for *Chicken Soup for the Soul.* Holy jamolies, right?!

You put out your first book, then you have a second book,

and you have all these truly amazing things happening. You have your very first book signing. How exciting is that?! I believe that would be October 16—I want you to remember that date. You are going through your life, going to different events and speaking at these events. You are meeting tons of people, and one of the beautiful things about meeting all these people in your life is ninety-nine percent of the time, you have no idea who these people are. They are just people who showed up in your life. You really like not even knowing who they are in the world and what they do for a living. Again, my friend, I want you to remember that is going to be another one of your superpowers.

You put your pants on the same way as everyone else. You don't find your friends because of who they are or what they do for a living. You have beautiful energy, and you always keep it in that state of mind. You can keep attracting beautiful, amazing people, because as much as I hate to tell you this, you are who you surround yourself with.

You are going to go through a period in your life where you are not even going to know who you used to be. You are not going to drink for a long time—not that there is anything wrong with drinking. This is something you wanted to do to clean up your health and the program you were on did not allow alcohol. You liked not having alcohol for a long time. You don't drink for several years. In this time, you meet this person and that person, you are taking this journey and that journey. You open up another studio, you open up three other businesses, and then somehow, some way, you become a producer of a film. You supported friends. You didn't support anyone *because* of anything. You supported them because you were with a group of people in an alternative club doing a project. You just showed your support. That was all.

You helped out at the event a little here and there, and the next thing you know, eight years later (October 16), you are sitting in Los Angeles on the red carpet for a film premier that you are an associate creative producer for. You want to know who that film is based upon? It is based around Jack Canfield's *Chicken Soup for the Soul.* Patty Aubrey, Jack's business partner; Jack Canfield; your publisher and beautiful friend, Kate Butler; and Dr. Angela are talking about their journey and all the things that have happened along the way with writing a book. It is amazing. You are sitting at a red-carpet premier, getting the paparazzi attention; pictures are being taken in a room full of all these amazing people. Then, you stand up with the microphone in hand and you are speaking. You are not even going to realize this is such a pivotal moment in your life. As you are talking, you see some of your closest friends sitting in the crowd, crying for you. It was just an ordinary moment that became an extraordinary opportunity.

Always remember to see the good in everyone. You have the divine ability to see things in people that they can't see in themselves. You are going to help a lot of people go through a lot of things in their life, and you are also going to help a lot of people start businesses. I just need to warn you on a few things. Not everyone is going to be grateful. Keep that in mind. So don't get your heart broke when people betray you. It is just part of the process.

Don't date anyone's potential. You see, a little bit of your downfall is that you date the potential instead of dating what is. You are going to date some incredible men. I want you to hold to holding out and not getting married because everybody else is getting married. You hold true to what is divinely yours, what you need, and what you want in your life. People are going to give you a hard time. People are going to do a comparison. You be divinely you. Realize you are enough just being you! You chose not to get married when society says you should by a certain age and not to have children—it is okay! Do not compare yourself to others. Even though you biologically won't have your own children, you will have so many children. So many people are going to call you Mom or their Chicago mom, and you are going to be a mom to a whole lot of animals who never want to leave you. Date accordingly. Always see the divine in everyone, and when you find something that interests you, make sure that you find so much interest in it that it is something you want to teach to others. There is a gift in that as well.

In *Chicken Soup for the Soul,* Jack said sometimes you have to let go of something that is really good in order to allow yourself to have something that is really great. You start to cry because you know—you *know*—that you are in a really good place in your life. You have a lot of great things happening, but you also know that on the other side of that good is great. You give yourself permission to step into that greatness. That little girl who people think is weird and different has all these gifts, intuition, sense of just knowing, déjà vu moments, channeling the indigo, and you realize that you can let go of something really good because you didn't base your identity on that. You just based that really good stuff on something that your heart was being called to do. You thought that was part of your purpose. But now, my love, get ready because your greatness is going to happen even bigger than it already was. I'm going to leave you with that—that little moment of realization, and then we are going to write the next chapter, the next book, the next novel, and I can't wait to tell you all the beautiful, natural things that are going to happen in your life.

Love, Older Self

ABOUT JODIE BAUDEK

Jodie Baudek is an inspiration to the masses. She will forever be the little angel on your shoulder talking you through life's many challenges. Jodie is best known as an entrepreneur, a highly sought-after keynote speaker, wellness coach, creative producer, best-selling international author, and the founder of Essence of Life Integrative Wellness Studios. In 2019, Jodie had the honor of being named the "Inspirational Woman of Chicago" award winner by Global Woman Co. She pours love, gratitude, inspiration, and self-confidence into others through her online coaching programs, YouTube channel, podcasts, and guided meditations. Jodie has been blessed in life to share the stage as a speaker alongside her mentors, and has been honored with the chance to interview some of the industry's top influencers such as Dr. Demartini, Lisa Nichols, Dr. Love, Don Miguel Ruiz Jr., and many more for her YouTube channel "Essence of Life with Jodie Baudek." After starting her career decades ago as a teacher in various healing arts, she now shares her passions and knowledge by leading the next generation to greatness through her accredited school.

YOU'LL SEE!

Tracey Watts Cirino

Dear younger self,

I'd like to congratulate you for being here. I have a tremendous amount of respect for the work you have put into being here, and I don't take that lightly. You have been so strong and courageous, and I would like you to know how much I love and respect you now and at every stage of your journey. Just curious, did you know the more you learn to trust yourself, the happier you will be? This has been proven time and time again when it comes to our mental and emotional health and well-being. It's important to note that self-trust is a complex and multifaceted construct that can be influenced by a variety of factors, and research is ongoing to better understand the complexity of self-love and trust. The more we know, the better we can do.

One of the ways we achieve personal joy and fulfillment is by getting to know ourselves and learning how to trust ourselves. The more we can stay present in this moment, the more trust we build with ourselves and others. That is why I have two very important secrets to share with you.

One is that you know and trust with every fiber of your being that you will find your people and build your tribe. Number two is that you will make the world a better place.

Now I know you might be asking yourself, *Why should I trust you?* I understand your concern, and it's like this: When you go to your favorite salon to get your hair colored, especially getting those gray hairs covered, you sit for about thirty-five minutes and you trust it to be complete, right? You will have no gray and your hair will be the beautiful color you expected to see. Your need for connection and waiting for that right big thing or that big moment is coming, and it is guaranteed when you believe and trust that it will be delivered. You will learn, when you surround yourself with negative people looking for what is wrong in the world instead of what is right, you will get a whole lot of what you don't want, and it will drain your energy and even make you angry. These are not bad people, they just believe that the world is conspiring against them instead of the whole universe looking out for them and guiding the way. Yes, the world is conspiring *for* you and wants to give you everything you ask for. You will try to force yourself into the boxes and labels so many others are trying to fit you into. You will discover that many things just don't fit well.

Eventually when you surround yourself with people who inspire you and empower you to become the best version of yourself, your world will grow and expand in bigger and better ways than you had ever thought or imagined. I promise you, this is where things get really good and juicy, and you really embrace all the joy and fun that life has to offer. You'll see!

You will become a four-time #1 international best-selling author. You will be an award-winning business owner and one of the most sought-after speakers and trainers on the planet. You will have two amazing kids and a loving, kind husband who supports and encourages your hopes and dreams. They will be your whole world, and you will have amazing moments of being fully aligned with your life's purpose and mission helping women business owners and entrepreneurs all around the world grow beyond what is common and break that million-dollar mark. You will be called the millionaire maker and help so many others build the life of their dreams.

Now it won't be easy until you decide you want it to be. You may feel like a weirdo upside down on the monkey bars—like nobody gets you and you are isolated and alone—but you will have to trust me here because you will find your people, build your tribe, and make the world a better place the *moment you trust yourself enough to truly be yourself.* You'll see!

Early in your career journey, you will struggle. This is a struggle of your own doing, waiting for this one big moment. You have always known you were meant for something big, you were meant for something huge, but at the beginning, you wait around for this big thing, this big moment, until one day you learn to get inspired and take any action. The small suburban street that you were born into makes you feel small right now, and they don't understand your creativity and need to hang upside down on the monkey bars when everyone else is doing the monkey bars the "right" way.

You need to trust that you will find your tribe the more you lean into loving yourself and being true to yourself. When you *trust yourself enough to be yourself,* you will start to see true magic transpire in your life and in your business. One of the things that you will discover along the way is that trust and worthiness go hand-in-hand. One of the biggest lessons you will learn is to *stop* breaking promises and agreements with yourself. The more you keep promises you make with yourself and develop self-discipline and trust, the more confidence you will have in all areas of your life. For years, you will believe many things that are not true and then one day you will see that light and discover your inner truth. You were not born to be a snoozer, and you can function in the morning without hitting snooze. In fact, your mornings will be so much better without it. What you eventually see and understand is that making yourself a priority and keeping agreements that you make with yourself like saying you will work out in the morning and then hitting snooze is what breaks trust with yourself and starts your day off on a negative broken promise to yourself.

Your whole world will change. With this one simple shift of making your needs and your mornings a priority, you will start building trust with yourself every day simply by making your needs a priority. Once you commit to your morning routine and what time you will wake up every day. Every day you *keep that commitment to yourself,* you will build and strengthen the bond of trust that you have with yourself to start your day off on the right foot. You will believe something so different for many years, then once you invite in curiosity and open yourself up to the possibility of thinking differently, you will build this first critical layer of trusting yourself. Once you realize that you get to set yourself up for the win, this part is in your control: trusting your word and keeping this promise to yourself, you will begin to develop the muscle of self-trust. Even when someone totally cuts you off on the way to work, you will say, "God bless" instead of "Bleep! Bleep!" You'll see!

When you begin speaking on stage at a very young age instead of telling yourself that you have nothing to offer and no one cares what you have to say, you will discover when you shift and tell yourself a new story and plant positive seeds of encouragement in your own mind that you have valuable lessons to teach everyone who comes to your classes and trainings. You will hear how everyone that attends your workshops leaves with a valuable tool that they can take back to their business and start generating more income right away.

When you're starting out, you will help the salon and beauty industry so much you will teach salon owners and leaders valuable tools that they can take back to their salon and implement right away to improve their team culture and generate more money. When you tell yourself that every event you speak at is filled to capacity and is standing room only, you realize that it becomes your truth. You have so much to offer, and you get to help so many people build their confidence and trust themselves enough to write their own paycheck! Instead of telling yourself everything that is wrong, tell yourself everything that is *right,* and by doing this, you will not only help yourself, you will help so many others.

As you grow into your speaking and coaching skills, you will continue to make a positive impact and shine a bright light into the lives of so many people that you have the honor and privilege to serve. There will be work, and some of it will be hard, and you may feel like you're dragging yourself and everyone around you up the tallest mountain. There will be times when you will question if you can make it. You will be tired, exhausted, and you'll feel like you're drowning and starving all at the same time. And you still will take one more step up the side of that mountain, and it will be worth it. It will be so worth it for you because you will really learn to like yourself and eventually learn to love yourself wholeheartedly. Even the dark, scary, jagged edges that you used to be afraid to share with the world. In fact, you will often say, "I don't just love me, I like me now too. There was work involved in getting here, and I really like who I am and where I am in this beautiful, wonderful life that I have co-created." You'll see!

This is one of the main lessons you teach on stage and in your digital training programs and in your books and in your one-on-ones with your coaching and consulting clients. It's going to take work for you to become who you really want to be and who you've known your whole life you have been called to be and really born to be. *Learning to trust yourself is the magic of your inner knowing.* You will be blessed with so many amazing mentors, guides, and teachers along your journey. Be present. Listen with your whole heart and both ears, and you will see them.

When you trust yourself enough to be yourself, your people seek you out and find you. When you are surrounded by your tribe of like-minded women leaders, creative business owners, entrepreneurs, authors, and aspiring business owners looking to grow to the next level, that is when and where you truly shine. This is where you get to use your core genius in helping other women business owners see and reveal their own core genius. What woman leader do you know who doesn't need this level of support and encouragement mixed with clarity and the right strategy?

Pour value into your tribe so they can earn more money while working less so they can create their dream life instead of working more hours feeling stressed out and overwhelmed, accepting less than they deserve, and having no life. Instead of feeling stuck, unfulfilled, and a lack of fun and joy, lead the *Beyond* Common movement for women business owners to trust themselves enough to step into their personal power to be themselves. That is what the business world truly needs, and that is what will lead us all to prosperity, joyful connection, fulfillment, and harmony!

You'll see!

Is it possible that you see yourself in this story? That you know you were meant for more?

This story was written to remind every woman leader that we are in this together and your younger self wants you to find the support you need to not just survive but to thrive.

Are you looking for your tribe? If you are getting everything you want out of life and more, then you already know what I am talking about here. If you are not, then take your own empowered action and enroll in your free Trust Yourself Video Series traceywattscirino.com/trust or take massive action and join one of our programs in Beyond Common Business Academy.

With love and gratitude,

Tracey Watts Cirino

You will find your people, and you will make the world a better place!

ABOUT TRACEY WATTS CIRINO

Tracey Watts Cirino is a #1 international best-selling author, award-winning business owner, highly engaging motivational speaker, and podcast host of *Beyond Common Business Secrets*.

Tracey is dedicated to helping creatives and entrepreneurs succeed through her dynamic keynotes, retreats, and coaching programs. As the founder and CEO of Beyond Common Coaching & Training Company, she is a certified success and mindset coach, Canfield Success Principles trainer, and John C. Maxwell certified speaker, coach, and trainer. Tracey has developed the proven Beyond Common Success Method and the Beyond Common Business Method and spends her free time walking and cooking with her family and their adorable dog.

To connect with Tracey

www.traceywattscirino.com
traceywattscirino.com/trust
Facebook: Tracey Watts Cirino
Instagram: @traceywattscirino
YouTube: Tracey Watts Cirino
TikTok: @traceywattscirino
LinkedIn: Tracey Watts Cirino

More book titles from Tracey Watts Cirino

Beyond Common 12 Essentials for Success in Life and in the Workplace
The Winter Owl
Women Who Shine, "Light that Shines Bright"
Women Who Dream, "You Are Worthy"

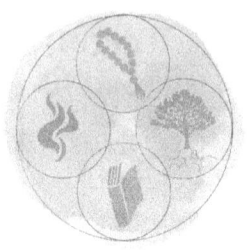

FINDING MY VOICE

Ellen Craine

"When you know and respect your Inner Nature, you know where you belong. You also know where you don't belong."

—Benjamin Hoff, *The Tao of Pooh*

Dear Ellen, I am sixty years old now, and I want to share with you, my younger self (and anyone else reading this who might need what I am sharing), how I got to the place I am today. It has not been easy to get here; there have been lots of twists and turns along the way. What I have learned is that life is not a straight line and there are no exact roadmaps that each one of us is supposed to follow. Instead, each one of us has a preordained roadmap influenced by life circumstances along the way that add to the twists and turns that show up expectedly and unexpectedly. I know I am still learning and growing from all of the twists and turns life continues to throw at me. Along the way, I have discovered that I am finding my voice bigger and stronger than I ever thought possible. The reality is that I will probably be working on this for the rest of my life on this earth. I have come to understand that finding my authentic voice is a life-long journey. It also means finding my inner nature and knowing where I do and don't belong. It means finding my passions and the real things and people that bring me joy and peace. It also means letting go of what does not. What follows are the steps that have gotten me to where I am today.

When I was a little girl, I remember feeling like I had a voice but not having permission to use it. Of course, others in my life might argue with me about this fact. What I remember was having feelings and thoughts and not being able to speak them out loud or feel like people wanted to really hear and see me for who *I* thought I was, not who they *wanted* me to be. Very quickly, I had to learn to stuff my feelings and not speak what I was thinking. I couldn't hate one of my sisters because I felt hurt and resentful of the way she treated me. I couldn't grieve my grandparents' deaths, or my mother's death. I was learning where I did not belong. I had a hard time finding things and people that brought me joy and peace or that I was passionate about. I had a hard time feeling like I belonged anywhere, and I did not know whom I belonged to.

However, what I know now that I wish I knew then, is that if we are not encouraged in all aspects of our lives, especially in sharing feelings, it is easy to lose our voice. We learn where we do not belong. We have trouble finding our joy, our inner peace, and the things we are passionate about. We do not know how to find our voice. It does not have to be this way.

It should be easy to feel like we belong. The reality is we all want to feel like we belong somewhere and with someone. Finding one's voice can help us get to that place of belonging, of feeling joy and peace. Most importantly, we need to feel like we belong to ourselves and can experience inner joy and peace. This can be done by finding one's voice.

When I refer to voice now, I refer to it in many different ways. A voice can be a vehicle through which we open our mouth and words come out, with or without music attached to it. We can have a speaking voice or a singing voice. Our voice can also speak to us and others via different art mediums: photography, painting, drawing, sculpting, chalk art, and the list goes on. The important point is to find our voice and feelings of belonging and use it in a way that is healing and supportive for us as individuals. We are each unique with our own individual voice, however we define it and use it.

How have I found my voice? I find my voice through walks in nature, working in my garden, reading, and journaling, to name a few. Finding my voice is just a piece of the puzzle. The other big piece is actually using my voice. I use my voice in a variety of aspects: in my teaching and consulting and in my counseling and coaching work. As I think about how I use my voice, I think about the fact that my goal is to facilitate authentic conversations by helping people find their voice, helping people live with and through their grief, and guiding people to find their inner light through any perceived darkness. These are all moments that matter in all of our lives.

Within the last couple of years, one way that I have found my voice is through writing and publishing chapters in books through the Impact Book Series with Kate Butler Books just like this one. This community, among many other support circles I have around me, has added to my sense of feeling like I belong somewhere with someone. It is an important tool for me finding my inner nature and knowing where I belong. My goal with my writing is to reach as many people as I can to support them in their lifelong journeys. I have always wanted to write and publish but did not feel confident or that I could really use my voice and follow through to completion until my first coauthored book, *Women Who Empower.* In my chapter in this book, I share about my journey as a pediatric cancer mom and becoming a widow after my husband's death from a Stage IV inoperable glioblastoma (a brain tumor) just six weeks after diagnosis. After this book was launched in December 2020, I thought I was done finding my voice. I had told my story. She was out in the universe, and I hoped I would impact even just one person. I was so scared when I wrote my chapter, "Living Through Loss and Grief," but I rose above my fear and did it anyway. I was proud that I actually finished it and got it published and into the world.

Then, I discovered I had another story to tell—or should I say, it found me. I was not planning on another chapter, but then life happened and gave me another story to share. In October 2020, I was diagnosed with breast cancer. During the course of my journey that first year, I knew I wanted to share my story to help at least one other woman who might find herself on a similar journey, even though I know no two journeys are exactly the same. In *Women Who Dream,* which launched July 2022, I wrote about the first year of my journey and how I walked through it by looking at each part of my diagnosis and treatment, including a double mastectomy, in phases with the help of my oncologist. My voice was starting to get louder, and I was continuing to feel more valued and empowered and that I could find my passion. I am happy to share that I just had a checkup with my oncologist, November 25, 2022, and I do not need to go back until May 2023. I will have a follow-up with my surgeon in January. I am confident I am healthy and living in vitality with a realistic goal of longevity.

Once *Women Who Dream* was launched, my voice was crying out to tell another story. I was invited to be part of the coauthored book *Leading with Legacy,* which launched October 26, 2022. In my chapter, "Finding the Light Through the Dark," I write about how we all go through dark times and that we all have light within us to help see us through. With the right tools, guidance, and support, we can all find our light. I want to help people find their light to help guide them through any darkness they may encounter.

I am grateful to say my son, Michael, the pediatric cancer patient at the age of eleven, is now a mostly thriving nineteen-year-old who also has a chapter in this book, *Dear Younger Self.*

I am honored and proud to see him finding a piece of his voice through sharing some of his thoughts, feelings, and experiences of his cancer journey and about the death of his dad, Marty. This is definitely not something he could do even six months ago, let alone when he was eleven years old. He also uses his voice through music. He loves listening to all kinds of music and finding meaning in the lyrics whether directly related to his own life or what is happening in the world around him. I am so proud of him (and I know his dad would be too) and the progress he is making in finding his voice. I am excited for everyone to read his chapter.

My older son, Matthew, has struggled with finding his voice. Perhaps he has had the hardest time of all of us because he lost his mom four different times at critical points in his life. He lost me, to a certain degree, when I was consumed with caring for Michael. He lost me again when my mom was terminally ill and I spent time away from him. Then, he lost me for a period of time when his dad was dying, and then again when I went through my breast cancer treatment. How does a twenty-three-year-old find their voice after all that?

Today, Matthew's voice is getting stronger. He is sharing more of his feelings, and he continues to work to find his passions in life. He is a college graduate with a degree in psychology. He has a job working in a research lab at a university. He continues to work toward figuring out what his passion really is and how to make that happen. Matthew loves sports and may even combine these two passions—sports and psychology—into a career that he is passionate about and brings him inner belonging, joy, and peace. I am so proud of him and the man he is becoming, and I know his dad, Marty, is very proud of him, too, even though he is not physically here to show it.

I have always tried to talk to my kids about finding their own voices or paths in life that are right for them. I always want them to be who they are meant to be and not who they think others want them to be. In addition, I have always tried to encourage my sons to talk about their grief. Some days are easier than others, and I need to remind even myself that this is a lifelong journey.

Dear Ellen (and anyone who is reading this), it is always important to use one's own voice and work on not letting others' opinions matter. Remember that finding and knowing our own inner nature is the most important tool for finding joy and peace. It is important to listen to our own voice first. When there is a passion to share your voice with others, however *voice* is defined to you, your voice will be heard by those who need to hear it. If someone doesn't or can't hear your authentic voice, it is often more about them and less about you; it is not the right time for them to receive what gifts you have to share. The way you speak, they may need to hear it another way. It may take multiple times of them hearing it before they can receive it.

Today, I use my voice to facilitate authentic conversations with and between others around the lifelong journey of loss and the collective reactions we call grief. I believe that having my voice stifled as a child and at different times throughout my life has contributed to this becoming one of my life purposes now. I have learned that the only way to find my voice is to keep using it. Every time I do, I find more of my voice and more of the gifts I have to offer to others and the universe. One way to use your voice is to reach out for guidance and support on your life journey. I am here for you. I hear you. I see you. I want to help you find more of your voice. Thank you for letting me help you through this chapter. I look forward to helping you even more as we share more with each other. You can reach me by email at ellen@crainecounseling.com. I would love to hear from you.

ABOUT ELLEN CRAINE

Ellen Craine, JD, LMSW, ACSW, INHC, is a social work ethics and grief expert in private practice. She has over 25 years of experience and is an effective trainer and educator. You can see a full list of her offerings and upcoming events, along with guest appearances, at www.crainecounseling.com.

Ellen is a #1 international best-selling author in Women Who Empower, Women Who Dream, and Leading with Legacy. She believes we need to have more authentic conversations around our life journeys and transitions, particularly loss and grief. Most struggles people face have roots in losses they have experienced. With loss comes various reactions we collectively call grief. Working through grief reactions can help facilitate a successful life journey and finding the light that exists in all of us. With an integrative wellness approach to healing, Ellen is passionate about empowering others.

Ellen loves spending time with her sons, pets, and friends. She also enjoys knitting, ceramics, yoga, walks in nature, meditating, and journaling.

She is the mother of a pediatric cancer survivor and a widow. She overcame breast cancer and is now considered a survivor. You can learn more about Ellen Craine and reach out to her to schedule workshops, trainings, or individual or group work on her website.

To connect with Ellen

www.crainecounseling.com
ellen@crainecounseling.com
Facebook group: Living Through Loss and Grief
Facebook page: Craine Counseling and Consulting Group
LinkedIn: Ellen Craine

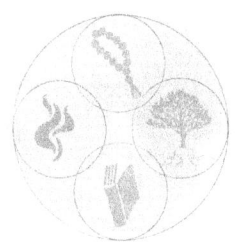

LIFE CAN THROW YOU CURVE BALLS YOU NEVER SAW COMING

Michael Rostker

Dear Michael (and anyone that needs to read this): Life can be hard and throw you all kinds of curve balls that you never saw coming. It's how you make it through those curve balls that helps you to become the person you are today and who you are meant to be. Here is my story in the hopes that it helps you, the reader, even in some small way.

Children often have wild dreams of what they want to be when they are older. Some dream of being astronauts; some want to be a doctor; and some a pilot. For me, I did not know what I wanted to be when I grew up. All I knew was that I wanted to do something that I enjoyed and had fun with. As a ten-year-old, I had no idea what it was that I enjoyed and had fun doing other than the "normal" kid things: LEGO and building things, when I wasn't exhausted or feeling poorly. I had trouble putting my joys and desires into words. I struggled with finding my voice. Throughout much of my youth, I did not know for sure if I would be able to make any of my dreams come true.

Before I talk about that, I have to take you back in time. I did not have a normal childhood. My mom and dad tried to give me that, but I ended up having a lot more doctors and medical issues than the average child. It all started when I was about six months old and a doctor noticed that my eyes did not look right. They ran some tests and I ended up needing eye surgery by the time I was one. Today I am close to being legally blind in my left eye, and I wear really strong prescription glasses. My mom nursed me as an infant, and I would always throw up during and after. As I got older, I told my parents that things did not feel right to me. Some of the symptoms were bad migraines, fatigue, night sweats, and I started losing my teeth earlier than normal. These are just some of the things I remember.

I started kindergarten at Oakland Steiner School (a Waldorf school) with my brother who was four years ahead of me. We were there until the beginning of my second grade. I did not have the greatest time there; I was blamed for starting a fight that I tried to stop. At that point, my parents decided we should switch schools.

We then transferred to Rudolf Steiner School (another Waldorf school) in Ann Arbor, which was a forty-five-minute drive from where we lived at the time. My time there was better and I had some new friends, but I was still seeing doctors.

By the time I turned ten, my symptoms had escalated. My mom took me to a genetics doctor to see if he could figure out how all of the struggles I was having might fit together. This doctor recommended that I see a hematologist/oncologist (a blood and cancer doctor). We saw one at Mott Children's Hospital at the University of Michigan. After a few tests, he sent us home and told us he would call with the results. When he finally called, he told my mom that they knew there was something wrong with me but that I was not sick enough for them and to come back if things got worse. Boy, did he fuck up!

In February, a couple of months shy of my eleventh birthday, my family and I went on a vacation that included a Disney Cruise followed by a trip to Disney World in Florida. We were there for approximately a week and even got to swim with the dolphins. I don't remember much else from the trip, but I remember feeling much worse than I had before, and at one point, I could not walk.

In April, I saw our family doctor in Ann Arbor, Dr. McMullen. During the appointment, he had heard a heart murmur that was not there before. He made the recommendation to see a cardiologist. He did not know that by hearing the heart murmur and recommending that I be seen by a cardiologist, he had saved my life. My mom acted like a good Jewish mother and got the earliest appointment she could with the cardiologist.

The appointment was not until May 14, a three-week wait and one day after my eleventh birthday. When we got there, they ran some standard tests. They did an EKG and an ultrasound of my heart, then we met with Dr. Cutler. She confirmed the heart murmur, but she also found fluid around my heart. She recommended that I be admitted immediately to the hospital to find out what was going on. Dr. Cutler told my mom that she did not know how I was standing, let alone walking. *Oh shit!!*

After we left the exam room, I was given a wheelchair to ride in. My mom and I were escorted with a nurse through underground tunnels to the pediatric intensive care unit (PICU) at Beaumont Children's Hospital. They did not know what was causing the fluid build-up, but it was life threatening. Almost every specialist in the hospital ran tests on me. I had multiple blood tests and multiple scans. After a couple of scans, they found a mass behind my heart. I am not sure what I was thinking or feeling back then, but thinking back now, my reaction is: *Are you fucking kidding me!?* Talk about life throwing me curve balls that I did not see coming. After they found the mass, the doctors and nurses had a pretty good idea of what it was, but they had to do a biopsy of the mass to be sure. The doctors had a hard time figuring out what the mass was because my body started to fight it, and it was already part scar tissue.

Once we got the test results back, they confirmed what

everyone was already thinking; it was diffuse large B-cell lymphoma: cancer. Fuck! The doctors immediately started me on steroids to try and bring the fluid down. They could not start the chemotherapy until the fluid had decreased or was completely gone. I was in the PICU for a total of eight days. During this time, I could not get out of bed or go to any tests outside of my room without being accompanied by a nurse and lots of equipment attached to me. I was confined to bed with little to do but listen to music and watch TV. No visitors were allowed but for immediate family and a couple of very close family friends.

At the end of the eight days, the doctors said they would have to drain the fluid from around my heart because the steroids were not working. They did not want to move me because I was so unstable due to the fluid impacting my heart functioning, so they did the surgery in my hospital room. They ended up removing ten ounces of fluid from around my heart, but they could not get it all.

Later that week, I had another procedure to check my spinal fluid for cancer. Thankfully there were no cancer cells present. Once my chemotherapy regimen was started, part of the protocol included the removal and testing of spinal fluid at the beginning and end of every round of treatment. After the spinal fluid was removed, they would inject chemo into the spinal fluid area to prevent cancer cells from landing there as the tumor near my heart dissolved. Each round of chemotherapy included me staying in the hospital for eight days.

The first time they did the procedure, they replaced my IV with a PICC line. A couple of days later, I told my mom and the doctors that my arm was hurting. They ended up doing an ultrasound of my arm. Following the ultrasound, the doctors told us that the cause of my pain was from a blood clot and that I would need emergency surgery to replace the PICC line with a medical port (which goes under your skin in your chest and makes it easier to receive the medicine you need). I wondered how many more curve balls life was going to throw at me.

My parents had not told me that I had cancer yet because they were worried about how I would react. Part of the concern was that a friend of my brother's had died from a different type of cancer a couple of years before, and it was traumatic for the whole family. So, when an ultrasound technician asked me, "How long have you had cancer for?" I had no idea what to do with this new curve ball I had just been thrown.

After the eight days in the PICU, I was moved into a normal hospital room. I was in the hospital for a total of two weeks in the beginning when they said that I could go home for a couple of days and then come back a few days later for my next round of chemotherapy. My mom and the doctor agreed it would be easier on me if I just stayed. After that stay in the hospital, which lasted a total of three weeks, I got to go home for a couple of weeks. The normal protocol was that I was supposed to be in the hospital for about eight days then come home for a couple of weeks with regular outpatient check-ups in between. Life kept throwing me curve balls, and I was almost never home for more than a few days before I had to go back to the hospital for one complication or another. There were strict rules that we had to follow. For instance, if I had a fever of 100.1 or higher, it was an automatic hospital admission. That happened almost every time I got to come home. It was really hard on me, my brother, and my parents.

During my time in the hospital, I was given an iPad, which I used to watch YouTube. When I was watching YouTube, I watched whatever looked interesting to me. What really caught my eye was a YouTuber who goes by the name JeromeASF. He plays Minecraft with his friends and sometimes other games as well. Watching YouTube, and in particular, JeromeASF, became a way for me to try to cope with the curve balls that kept getting thrown at me.

Later on during my treatment, I heard part of a song written and performed by the rapper Eminem (2010) called "Not Afraid" that caught my attention. Once I heard the words, I fell in love with the song. I did not know it at the time, but I think I loved it so much because I had a sense that I could relate to it. In the song, Eminem talks about his drug addiction and getting clean, and he is trying to help anybody who is going through a similar situation or any difficult time or challenge.

Thinking about the lyrics to this Eminem song reinforces why I am sharing my story with you. I want to help you, my younger self and anybody else who is reading this who finds themselves in a challenging life situation. I want you to know that life can throw you curve balls, and it is important to find ways to cope that are healthy and lead you to a better place.

September 1, 2014, was my first day off treatment, but I would still need antibiotic infusions weekly at the outpatient pediatric cancer center at the hospital where I was treated. The protocol was that it would have to be at least five years of showing no evidence of disease before I was declared cancer-free. As of September 1, 2022, it has been nine years and I am proud to say that I am cancer-free!

During that five-month period in the hospital, I was not able to go back to school. Once my treatment was complete, I had so many complications that my mom ended up homeschooling me until my freshman year of high school. When I started high school, I was not able to go full-time due to my extreme fatigue. I was diagnosed with a mitochondrial disorder as one of the complications of the chemotherapy I received. The school tried to help me with what I missed, but I really struggled and had a rough two years there. After my sophomore year, it was clear that they could no longer help me.

My mom had me get some neuropsychological testing to see what learning challenges I had, if any. I was diagnosed with dyslexia and dysgraphia; basically, I have horrible writing skills. I am now in my senior year at a special school that helps students with learning challenges, and I am on track to graduate this year, June 2023.

During my time in and out of the hospital, I never really knew how to express myself. I did not allow my friends to visit me in the hospital, and I never wanted to go anywhere when I was home. All I wanted was to stay home and watch TV. More recently, I have realized that it was just a way for me to escape so I did not have to think about all the shit happening to me and my family.

Two years into my recovery, my family and I thought we were done with medical problems; boy were we far from wrong! At about this time, February 2016, we were in the process of moving when my dad fell and hit his head. My mom took him to the emergency room to make sure he did not have a concussion. When they got there, they ran some tests and the hospital eventually released him and said there was nothing up there.

During the following weeks, he started to get much worse, so my mom took him to a different hospital emergency room. They ran a more thorough scan of my dad's head and found a mass in his brain. They were able to do a biopsy of the mass and found out it was a Stage IV inoperable glioblastoma. The doctors said that because of where the tumor was, removing it by surgery was not an option. The only option to possibly prolong his life was chemotherapy and radiation. I could not fucking believe that my family and I were being thrown another curve ball.

After doing research, my mom requested that he be transferred to another hospital that had the best neurology program. My dad was transferred. At the new hospital, they wanted to look at the tissue themselves that was taken at the previous hospital to come to their own conclusions about the type of cancer my dad had. Unfortunately, they came to the same conclusion as the first hospital did. My dad started to get worse even before they could start the chemotherapy and radiation. After about five weeks, it was clear that the treatments were not working.

My dad was in the hospital for a total of six weeks before he passed away. One day when I went to visit him, about a week before he died, he told me, "Take care of Shayna" (our dog) and "I love you, Michael." I did not know it at the time, but those were his last words to me before he died. I had no words at the time to describe how I was feeling and what I was thinking.

If I could tell you, younger Michael, anything to help you, it would be to not be afraid to use your voice to share how you feel. When you do not use your voice, you keep everything locked up inside and it makes it harder to function and be the best that you can be. I am still working on finding my voice. It is still hard for me to process all the curve balls I have been thrown, everything I have been through, but I am learning new ways every day. Writing is one way for me to get my feelings out. Listening to music is another tool I use. I like listening to songs and thinking about what they mean and how they apply to my life.

Life is filled with curve balls that can come at you fast and furious. It is okay not to know how to deal with them at the time. What is important is to know that they happen and that you have some internal coping skills to help get you through. Through surviving these curve balls, it is possible to learn new coping skills that work and make you stronger for the next curve balls. In spite of the curve balls you face, never give up on your dreams, and get the support you need to help you get there.

ABOUT MICHAEL ROSTKER

Michael Rostker is currently a student at Ann Arbor Academy. He plans to go on to college after he graduates. While he is unsure of what he wants to study, he is looking forward to the opportunity to continue to find his voice and follow his dreams.

Michael currently lives at home with his mother. He loves to spend time with his older brother playing disc golf and doing other brotherly things. Another passion of his is listening to music and sometimes creating his own.

To connect with Michael

michaelrostker@gmail.com
Facebook: Michael Rostker

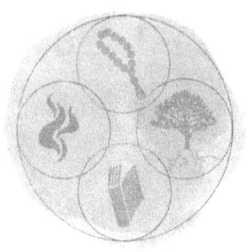

NURTURING THE NOW

Mary Helen Gervais

It had been a crazy day, and I was mentally reviewing my to-do list while activating the bakery's alarm system. We opened at 6 a.m. and closed at 2:30 p.m., so I could easily jump in my car and pick up the kids at school when we had after-school activities planned. I had fifteen minutes to make it to school and then we had thirty minutes of quality time before their music and movement class. As an entrepreneur and busy mom with a kindergartner and second grader, timing was everything.

Zooming onto the busy highway, I heard sirens and quickly realized a state trooper was flagging me to pull over. My first thoughts: "Why is he stopping me? It's just going to make me late." It became immediately clear that this feisty, towering trooper was not happy. I had supposedly cut him off upon entering the highway and then immediately merged two lanes to the left to connect to my interstate. He drilled me. "Where was I coming from and where was I going, and why was I in such a rush?" Fortunately, after I apologized, he let me off without a ticket, but his stern warning included a lecture about how easy it was to have an accident when you're not fully present in the moment. *Hmm . . .* I thought. *You have no idea how chaotic and fast-paced life can be.*

Life *is* busy, right? We live in a changing world, we have instant access to information, and we juggle multiple priorities and plates in the air. But my exchange with the state trooper did make me stop to consider how I needed to give myself some additional time to make it to where I was going. However, the full impact of that moment wouldn't arrive for some years.

My children are now in their early twenties, but shortly after selling my bakery, when my son and daughter were nine and eleven years old, it hit me that any chaos in my life was not a good thing. At that point, I began to notice and even accept that if my drive was interrupted by a train or road work or a red light, it was meant to be. This momentary pause was a gift. It gave me time to center myself, take a breath, or enjoy the surroundings. The importance of harmony and balance started to resonate with me.

It was at this juncture that I started down the road to true self-discovery. Of course, we don't wake up one day and go, "Aha, this is who I am." It takes many "aha" moments and experiences for us to discover who we are at the core.

My pre-entrepreneurial days in corporate America graced me with wonderful training and many useful books such as *The 7 Habits of Highly Effective People* and *Who Moved My Cheese?* As I continued down the self-discovery path, attending seminars about mind, body, and health connections, family systems and relationships, and work and money synergies, my reading extended to such books as *The Alchemist*, *The Four Agreements*, and *The Celestine Prophecy*.

In the search for validation, permission, and love, we ultimately need to realize that everything we need is within us. Things happen for us, not to us. The journey truly is about how we come to know, trust, and honor ourselves.

To *be* means allowing yourself to exist as you are in the present moment. Forget the past and don't fret about the future. You are exactly where you need to be at this moment. When we do this, the magic happens.

A few years ago, I facilitated a Grow Your Business seminar with a group of rockstar women entrepreneurs. The ten-week course encompassed how to develop a strategy for taking a business to the next level while also harnessing the group's energy to create synergy for collaboration, expansion, innovation, and deep professional connections. I also asked the women to reflect on three experiences that made them who they are today. I added three of my own experiences to the discussion.

Jumping in Feet-First

At ten, I knew I wanted to be a foreign exchange student when I reached high school. My parents' stories and photographs from their time living and working in Europe when they were first married, coupled with childhood travels, adventure books, and the *National Geographic* opened my eyes to the world. Family friends also had a foreign exchange student staying with them. He was super cool, and I loved the sense of adventure that he talked about. To this day, I believe that my burning desire to travel is my soul's longing to grow.

At fifteen, I was selected by Rotary International to represent my local Rotary club, my community, and the US. After training for a year, my departure date for Johannesburg, South Africa, was eight weeks away. But the country's internal resistance to apartheid made travel there unsafe, and Rotary called to tell me that all student exchange programs in SA had been canceled for the year. I was promised a country placement within a week's time.

It seemed like ages, but before the week was up, I was given a placement in Oruro, Bolivia, high up in the Andes Mountains. I was so excited and couldn't wait to research my new destination in *The World Book Encyclopedia* and at the library. My heart felt alive, and I was only slightly questioning the fact that my second language studies had been French, not Spanish.

I still remember boarding my Braniff Airlines flight from JFK to the Bolivian capital LaPaz. Everyone was speaking Spanish, and it felt overwhelming. After striking up a few conversations with the flight crew who spoke perfect English, I felt more relaxed.

The drive from LaPaz to Oruro takes four hours along steep mountain switchbacks; the altiplano is beautiful. I stared in awe at the majestic mountains and women in brightly colored skirts, straw hats, and jewelry who were herding their alpacas and llamas. My host dad, Emilio, spoke a little English, so between my pocket dictionary and his few words, I began to settle in for the drive to my new home. I was shocked when we stopped for lunch and the restroom was a glorified outhouse. Fortunately, I recalled the word, *humility*, from my Rotary pre-departure training.

Language immersion is an intense, heavy workout, and I'd get huge headaches by midafternoon. It took three months for me to understand conversations and six months to speak without hesitation. But, by the year's end, I was able to think and converse fluently in Spanish.

I did not know it then, but the universe was truly guiding me. The magic of flow—or the freedom I experienced by letting go—allowed me to grow. Life that year was beautiful, meaningful, and fun. The opportunity made me wiser, and the more I understood the depths of my ignorance, the more I gained a sense of humility, reverence, and respect for others.

When we look back at certain moments in life, we don't always understand why or how we got there. But one thing is certain: There are no random happenings. My younger self did not know that this experience in Bolivia would bring incredible bilingual job opportunities and insight into other languages, along with the confidence to travel the world and explore other cultures.

Dear younger self, you should know that when everything is changing, it's a new beginning that will amplify your life in countless ways. Jump on board and ride the wave.

Playing Havoc on My Body

After graduating from college, I spent the summer working on Martha's Vineyard before heading off to start my professional career in New York City. I am a nature lover and an avid runner. My father's home had direct access to the island's bike route, and I frequently ran along the soft dirt path next to it.

In July I came down with terrible fatigue and flu-like symptoms. Used to doing energetic five- to seven-mile runs, I couldn't figure out why the flu-symptoms persisted. My doctor explained that Martha's Vineyard was a haven for ticks and Lyme disease. But there was no evidence of a bull's eye rash, which is generally what a tick bite area looks like, and I tested negative for Lyme. So after another week's rest, I went back to my waitressing job. But I was still thoroughly exhausted. Returning to the doctor's office, he ran another test. It also came back negative. He explained that positive results often only show up in a small percentage of actual Lyme infections. So, erring on the side of caution, he prescribed an antibiotic treatment plan. I felt better but did not get back to normal until summer's end.

When a friend invited me to join him on a trip to Mexico, I jumped at the opportunity. We landed in Mazatlan, rented a car, and explored the coast. It was a great trip until the last two days when my friend, JJ, came down with a fever. By the time we returned to the States, we were both sick. The diagnosis: hepatitis A. After reconstructing the timeline, we realized that it was most likely from contaminated raw shellfish that we had eaten along the Mexican coast.

Havoc is a good word to describe what was happening to my body at that point. Lyme disease weakens the immune system, and hepatitis A is a virus that causes irritation and swelling of the liver. Fever, fatigue, and nausea kept me in bed for weeks. By late December, I was getting my strength back, but I was in terrible pain every time I ate. A battery of tests was run. They all came back normal. As I was trying to figure out my next step, JJ invited me to spend some time with him and his family in Colorado. I accepted and departed for Denver.

During my time in Colorado, I enrolled in a six-month travel certification program. My stomach pain and fatigue lessened but persisted, and I went to the hospital for additional extensive testing. Everything came back normal, and I recall one physician asking me if I was a hypochondriac.

Determined to get better, I kept searching to find a team of health advisers to help heal me, not fix me. This is when I came across holistic medicine. In the late 1980s, healing aimed at improving health and wellness through the body, mind, and soul was still in its nascent stage. After we completed a full workup of tests for metals and minerals, it was determined that my system was completely out of whack. What followed was a strict three-month diet of fresh vegetables, chicken, eggs, quinoa, oats, and soy milk along with liquid vitamins and minerals. My energy started to return, and I began to take long walks, to swim, and work with a Reiki practitioner. At twenty-three, this experience was an eye-opener about the importance of exercise and healthy eating but also about mental and emotional balance.

Dear younger self, you should know that your health is much more than just your physical body and the absence of disease. True health comes when you are able to create harmony between your spiritual, mental, emotional, and physical bodies. Your body talks to you. Your energy system speaks to you. You must listen and act accordingly to achieve your best health.

Healing is not passive. We must own and commit to it. We must actively lead this personal journey of becoming our optimal selves. By showing up, going slow, and paying attention in present-moment awareness, my own energy began to flow and I healed. As you can see, taking care of the body includes taking care of the heart and mind.

Finding My Heart in Puerto Rico

One of my first jobs out of college was in sales and marketing for a Chilean airline. This was incredible as I was able to earn income and also travel the world. In my travels, I met my husband, Bobby, in Puerto Rico. He spoke limited English when we first met and his grandmother, Mama Minga, spoke no English. Having grown up with only one grandmother who passed away when I was in college, I cherished the time spent with my Mama Minga, a petite soul who embodied warmth, kindness, laughter, and love. Her stories, incredible cooking, and instant acceptance of me as the first non–Puerto Rican in the family were a gift and blessing.

Without my experiences in Bolivia so many years before, I would not have been able to communicate with Mama Minga, let alone create these beautiful moments with her.

Puerto Rico is an immensely beautiful island with a skilled, bilingual, and highly educated workforce. I moved to the island when I was twenty-seven. I planned to waitress until I found a professional job. Finding a waitressing job was easy. Finding a good corporate job was difficult—even with a résumé peppered with solid skills and achievements. Given the nature of being on an island, job openings were limited. I interviewed for at least twenty positions and would typically come in as a finalist, but then someone's son or cousin would have a connection to the company. Ultimately, landing a job through your network works. However, as an island newbie, my network was very small.

Finally, during a morning run one day, I remember saying to myself, "It's time to try a different approach." After pausing and listening to my inner voice, I regrouped and reached out to a headhunter. I was then referred to another recruiter who had a new posting working with a retail jewelry company. She thought I was a good fit. Having had some retail jobs in college, I moved forward with the interview process, but to be truthful I didn't know a thing about jewelry. After interviewing with the owner and her daughters who worked with her in their six stores, I was hired as the district manager for the island.

Little did I know that working with Marie Helene Reinhold

would be such a life-altering experience. The company had two divisions: Reinhold Jewelers, a designer jewelry concept that marketed the designer's brand name and work as art, and Daughters, a chain of stores with less expensive jewelry products. The Reinhold designers were exquisite and included designers like David Yurman, Michael Bondaza, John Hardy, Robert Lee Morris, Penny Preville, and many others. Reinhold had also acquired the exclusivity of Tiffany & Co. in Puerto Rico.

One of my favorite parts of the job was traveling weekly in Marie Helene's car as we visited the stores around the island and discussed business, jewelry, and our love of art and life. We had similar stories of falling in love with beautiful Puerto Rico and meeting our husbands on the island.

Marie Helene gave me a chance and saw a potential in me that I had not yet recognized. I loved how she nudged me to see things from a different perspective. One day, I wore an intricate, relatively inexpensive dragonfly marcasite pin. She raved about its beauty and continued the conversation by telling me to look at every piece of jewelry as art, whether it cost $15 or $60,000.

There were many times when she pulled me out of my comfort zone, such as the day she announced that I would lead and create a corporate training program for the staff. Having never done this, I gulped, rolled up my sleeves, and got to work. I was amazed at how it all came together. Marie Helene taught me the art of telling the story of a brand by establishing an emotional connection with people, by talking about the designer, their background, and what made the piece unique.

Sadly, after more than a year, the Daughters sales were not performing as planned and we closed the chain. It was painful to get things in order behind the scenes, but being fully prepared and then upfront and honest with the team made the process easier. Marie Helene also taught me to look at the closing as an opportunity to learn and grow. She took me under her wing and, as a true mentor, walked alongside me to show me what I could do. To this day, Marie Helene remains the most impactful mentor in my life. I am so grateful.

I share this with you, dear younger self. At times we are pushed, tested, and stretched by the events in our life. If you get frustrated and do not exactly like your current situation, this is when it's important to pause, lean back, and breathe. It's only human to want to be in control of everything. But when the universe sets up its periodic detours, sometimes your only option may be to surrender. Trusting divine timing is surrendering yourself to the guidance of the universe. It's believing that events will happen in your life at precisely the right time, no matter how long it takes.

When we are conscious, we can take the tempo down a notch and allow ourselves to *just be*. This opens up the space for change and for life to flow with ease and grace. In truth, we are the storytellers of our own lives. Give yourself permission to ease up and recognize that everything you seek is already inside of you. You just have to see it and choose to act upon it.

See you. Be you. And sing the beautiful song in your heart.

ABOUT MARY HELEN GERVAIS

Serial entrepreneur and innovator Mary Helen Gervais has helped thousands of women fulfill their dreams of starting, building, and growing their own companies.

Driven by a desire to create more meaningful connections between people and to make the world a more honest and open place, she has also established herself as a leader and guide in co-creation—a form of collaborative innovation where ideas are shared and improved together.

Thriving on new experiences, Mary's love of world travel has led her to live and work in Bolivia, Sweden, Spain, Chile, and Puerto Rico. She has used her marketing savvy and business acumen to create both retail and online enterprises, and she is the former head of Rhode Island's Women's Business Center.

Mary is also a firm believer in the idea that when life hands you a grand idea, embrace it, even if you don't know how to make it happen. Dream big and be bold. Leading by example, Mary continues to show others how to live an abundant, healthy, and joy-filled life.

To connect with Mary

www.maryhelengervais.com
mary@maryhelengervais.com

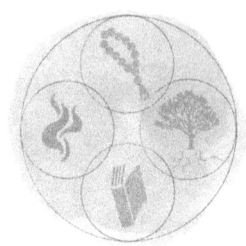

EVERYTHING IS GOING TO BE ALL RIGHT

Tiffany Donovan Green

Dear Younger Self,
Dry your tears. Set your troubles aside. Breathe. Do not retreat; stand tall. Now is the time for compassion and courage, not regret or self-pity. A metamorphosis is taking place. She may not realize it, but the child you see before you is about to embark on a one-of-a-kind adventure! She shall journey forth; she will begin to move through the wilderness with her mother's intuition, her father's generosity, her grandmother's grit, and the innocence of her lost brother. She will be guided by gracious and benevolent spirits. Her heart and mind will blossom. She will encounter mystery and magic. And she will find herself—a woman with capability and prowess, creativity and insight, purpose and intention.

I wish I could tell her that it's going to be easy, but I cannot. There will be heartbreak, grief, sacrifice, loss, anger, shame, anxiety, fear, strenuous labor, and failure; but there will also be joy, courage, determination, gratitude, generosity, wonderment, and genuine heartfelt love. In fact, in my experience, you can't have the good without bad because hardship provides the necessary lens from which our perception of beauty is derived. If every day was easy and abundant, we'd all be jaded, ill-prepared for inevitable setbacks, and unable to appreciate each other and the hidden treasures of this world.

I can't tell her with specificity the outcome of her life choices because the future is not set in stone. Her fate is unknown since the process is still unfolding. As she steps forward into the world, there will be so many paths from which to choose that even the benefit of hindsight could not unravel the would-be scenarios that will come to define her experience. As we age, we gain no magical power of foresight beyond what a good hunch and reasonable expectation are apt to provide. She must be content with uncertainty and trust in the universe.

What I *can* tell her is that everything is going to be all right. That's a bit of a spoiler, but when self-doubt invades, reassurance is imperative, for doubt will be the origin of her demons. When she was just a young child, the world came to rest on her shoulders; she had to take on tremendous responsibility, more than she should have at that age. She had to be strong, hold down the fort, and protect her loved ones. She had to become a caregiver, a problem-solver; she had to rise when those around her fell; she had to be steady in high wind and navigate crisis with sharpened wit and reinforced resolve. In her mind she had to become a superhero, red cape and all. Her shadow was long, but when the storm subsided, she dissolved. She became cognizant of her limitations. She had to accept that some things are beyond her control; she doesn't have all the answers. She is not invincible, only human. These experiences left her depleted, anxious, overwhelmed, and susceptible to the darkness in others. I'm here to tell her that everything is going to be all right, not because her life will be perfect and all her fantasies will materialize but because whatever will be, will be, and that's okay because she can handle it.

That said, I can share what my limited experience has garnered over the years, some ideas and suggestions to help her find her way when darkness descends:

Don't Overthink It. Trust your gut; you don't need to over-analyze and second-guess every decision. Have faith in your intuition and instincts. You will find that in most circumstances, there really isn't a right or wrong answer, simply variations on a theme. If you make a choice that leads you in an undesirable direction, pivot—or reverse course. Everyone moves through life with some degree of myopia; certainty is illusory. Don't worry about what others think; they have no more power over your thoughts than you have over theirs. Just be yourself, and if that's not good enough, then let them move on. Mistakes are forgivable, necessary even, assuming you attempt to learn from them.

Show Some Muscle. Lift weights, both literally and figuratively. Yes, you need to stay fit, but more importantly, you need to stay strong, and I'm talking about the kind of strength that comes with the ability to say no. Allowing others to take advantage could have an adverse effect resulting in imbalance and regret, which can be injurious to your character and your relationships. If you intend to be charitable, then you must do so on your terms with no expectation of reciprocity. Maintain appropriate boundaries.

Be Patient. Reflect before you react. There will be many situations in which you will be tempted toward a knee-jerk reaction. It could be useful to temper your response. Don't jump to conclusions; things aren't always what they seem. Often there is more at work than meets the eye. Try to put yourself in the shoes of others. Ask, *What is really going on?* If there is pain, what is the source and why are you the target of this individual's emotional turmoil? Building relationships is a lot like farming a crop. A successful gardener knows patience; if she desires a bountiful harvest, she plants healthy seeds and tends to them with meticulous care, utilizing her knowledge of soil and sun.

Get Smart. There is so much to learn. Stay educated. Pursue practical knowledge as well as academic expertise. Technological proficiency is intrinsic to modern life; embrace it. Wisdom is more ethereal but can be attained through a combination of spiritual guidance, mediation, observation, and reflection. Share your insights; teaching others is the first step toward true understanding.

Live in the Present Moment. Don't dwell on that over which you have no control. The past may provide sentimental comfort, but it has limited relevance. Don't anchor yourself to it, or you will be moored to a realm of ghosts and haunted by regret. Let go. Don't miss your chance to live in the here and now. Focus on the present with an eye toward the future. Feel your feet firmly on the ground but beware of rigidity. Put simply, go with the flow. Relax. Stay forward-facing, open to fresh opportunities and new directions. Pay attention to the ordinary—the small, unremarkable details that are so often taken for granted—and you will find gold. Staying present is an acquired skill; it might require a little practice. The future is a moving target, yet you can influence it by making rational choices such as eating healthy, exercising regularly, staying hydrated, employing financial prudence, investing in relationships, and staying informed.

Never Say Never. The universe has a strange way of making us eat our words. Don't be tempted into testing it. When you say *never*, *never* will invariably make an immediate appearance. We are all bound to the tutelage of an omniscient power that is alert to our foibles and seizes every opportunity to illustrate the depth of our ignorance. I believe this universal phenomenon is well intended and designed to expand understanding and aid our growth. When you inevitably fall prey to it, be mindful that it's a teaching moment and try to observe the lesson.

Stay Organized. Invest the necessary time and energy to keep important documents and communications, calendars, photographs, memorabilia, journals, academic projects, and instructions properly catalogued. Your memory will not always be as sharp as it is at present, and when you look back and ask, "Where did the time go?" you will be grateful that you have an accessible record to reflect on. It will be healthy for your mood and mind to keep your roots, achievements, celebrations, and victories fresh and alive.

Expect the Unexpected. The key to survival, on both a physical and emotional level, is adaptation. Maintain flexibility. Try to stay alert with a contingency plan at the back of your head that is accessible and adaptable. Winds can shift; sudden changes in health, employment, income, and economic conditions can impact you or a loved one. Plan for the future—make sensible investments in education, real estate, securities, and insurance. Take nothing for granted.

Practice the Golden Rule. Treat others the way you expect to be treated. Don't feel obligated to follow the herd, especially if that path violates your sense of righteousness. Stand up for the weak and weary. Give a helping hand to those in need even if it requires sacrifice. I have seen evidence of the axiom, "You only get what you give." Avoid passing judgment. You will learn that there is nothing more destructive than shame. Keep promises. If you are trustworthy, you can trust and be trusted.

Watch Your Words. Avoid victimization by using your voice, but be mindful about the energy your words put into the world. Examine your intentions before you speak and ensure proper alignment. Words spoken in anger cause more harm than good. Envision the desired outcome and calibrate your response accordingly. Reign in that Italian temper! Silence can be equally effective. Don't always surrender to keep the peace; when under attack, defend yourself by exposing the root of the issue: Always ask why. *What is really going on here?* Perhaps the perpetrator is projecting their insecurities onto you in order to process their own pain.

Seasons Change. Change is not only inevitable, it is often predictable. Plan for it. Know what to expect at each juncture in life. Your values, your needs, your interests, and your capabilities will continue to mutate as you progress from a teen to a responsible adult, from marriage to motherhood, from menopause to old age. Each transition brings with it an existential reckoning;

you will feel entirely different yet exactly the same. Maintain an open mind as you turn each corner. For the best results, maintain flexibility and lower expectations.

It Could Be Worse. Undoubtedly, you will encounter difficulties. Remain steadfast, and as the ancient adage goes, "This too shall pass." This was your mother's favorite maxim. Understand that it is natural to get down in the face of an unwelcomed challenge. Be kind to yourself. Seek solace, but do not dig too deep a hole; there is danger in darkness.

Face Your Fear. Easier said than done. Fear is complicated because it derives from multiple sources and coalesces in a dark cloud of distrust and uncertainty. But if you fail to face it, it will continue to grow unchecked. Avoidance is akin to acquiescence, and ultimate surrender. Unbridled fear thwarts forward momentum, derails character, and unravels the soul. Few know fear the way you do because you absorbed it at the earliest moments of life. At the conclusion of a healthy full-term pregnancy, Mother almost lost her life to a sudden hemorrhage caused by an undetected placental abnormality and medical malpractice. She was transfused with eight pints of blood, but her firstborn child could not be saved. Your older brother, our baby Timmy, died in utero. Her heart, her confidence, and her faith were shattered. But she was determined to bring life into the world, and you, baby girl, were eventually conceived. Unfortunately, given the trauma of prior events, you were bathed in anticipated misfortune, fear, distrust, and anxiety from the moment of inception; even after a successful delivery, your parents regarded every hiccup as a potentially life-threatening event. It was a rough start, but you no longer need to own the anxiety of others. If you welcome your fears rather than control them, you can defuse the mechanism by which rational cognition is subverted and limit their power. Exposure therapy works. Your inhibitions need not necessitate restraint.

You Can't Win 'Em All. You'll need to learn when to call it quits. You won't win everyone's approval. Don't take it personally.

There is a lesson in every failed relationship, which will guide you to greater happiness. Again, trust your instincts. We are animals and we can sense danger. Often you will feel betrayal before evidence of it has surfaced. You are not obligated to trust everyone; rather, let others earn your confidence and respect. Don't be fooled by flattery and false promise; not every heart is as pure as your own.

Follow the Light. Stay in alignment with your values and character. Darkness is deceiving. It can masquerade as regret, frustration, anger, self-pity, and shame. These are natural human emotions and thus not entirely avoidable, but don't let darkness drag you too deep. When you are feeling slighted or overwhelmed, concentrate on desired outcomes and reconnect with gratitude. You can give yourself permission to process negativity but set firm limits. Don't wallow. It's easy to get lost in dark places.

Laugh It Up. It's true. Laughter is the best medicine, particularly when you are the object of innocent mirth and witless sarcasm. Remember when you met your best friend in middle school. She had you in stitches for hours at a time; her observational sense of humor was at one with your appetite for self-deprecation. This dynamic of belonging bolstered your confidence and allowed you to bloom. Soon your circle grew to accommodate multiple forever friends who, over the remainder of life, will continue to reminisce about those youthful years of unforgettable hilarity. A good laugh goes a long way.

Be Perfectly Imperfect. The sooner you let go of the need for perfection, the better off you'll be. Impossible standards are unattainable. If you aim too high, you'll set yourself up for failure, which will dent your confidence and hold you back. You can still dream big and have realistic expectations. Approach missed marks as a learning opportunity or a source of inspiration, not as a commentary of deficiency.

Ask for Help. You don't have to go it alone. It's easy to think that to do it right, you need to do it yourself, but in reality, those who ask for help tend to be more balanced, more productive, and more successful. Think about it as teambuilding. Like your football-obsessed child will eventually say, "The quarterback can always try to run the ball, but more often than not, he makes a pass." Seek solid advice. Be selective. Guidance can come in various forms: courses, books, word of mouth, or from professionals in the field. The areas you will need the most guidance include career, finance, child-rearing, technology, medicine, and time management.

Dream Big! You are a creative with the ability to make your visions reality. Notwithstanding the need for practicality in most aspects of daily life—indulge in fantasy! This is your greatest gift. Use it! Let your imagination flow. Shoot for the stars. Close your eyes and dream. You have the power to bring fairy tales to life. Belief in magic will keep you young at heart.

It Pays to Discover. Everything comes at its own true price; all things of value must be earned. Accomplishments require sacrifice. To find out who you really are and what you are capable of, you must explore your boundaries, step outside your comfort zone, and challenge yourself. Learn what fits by trying on different hats. Don't get too comfortable or you will atrophy. Be open to new experiences and the lessons that follow to gain perspective and gratitude. It's going to be a wild ride, but you will survive each twist and turn if you face it head-on, eyes open.

Never Give Up! It's cliché, but there is no better way to say it: "If at first you don't succeed, try and try again." There will be times you will want to give up, hide, quit, or run away. While it may be wise to accept the eventuality of foreseeable outcomes, such circumstances need not necessitate unconditional surrender. It's never too late to right a wrong, make amends, or believe in yourself. The sun rises after the darkness of night. Spring follows the dearth of winter. Have faith in your ability to regain your stride after a stumble or a fall.

Be True to Yourself. You are an original. Don't be afraid to own it. Avoid boxing yourself in with artificial constructs and external expectations. Your gifts are unique. Your soul is a singularity. Allow your purpose to be self-directed and attuned to righteousness.

And that, in a nutshell, is my humble advice to date. I hope this counsel holds true. The one thing I know with certainty, is that in this moment, you are everything you need be to have a rewarding, purpose-driven life. Never lose sight of the ultimate goal—it's not fame or fortune that drives us but the desire to bring peace and happiness to those we love. The universe provides. Everything will be all right. Relax and enjoy the ride!

Bon Voyage!

ABOUT TIFFANY DONOVAN GREEN

Tiffany Donovan Green is an interior designer and event organizer, as well as an attorney specializing in international environmental law. She is the founder of The Green House Interiors, promoting healthy, sustainable design, and co-founder of two nonprofit organizations: The Tiara Club, a sisterhood of inspired women, and The Global Preservation Society, supporting environmental stewardship and sustainability. She is a #1 international best-selling author in *Women Who Dream*, the eighth book in the Impact Book Series with Kate Butler.

Born and raised in southeastern Michigan, Tiffany earned a BA in history and political science from Albion College, an MA in American environmental and cultural history at Oakland University, a JD/LLM in international and comparative law from Cornell Law School and is pursuing an MA in interior design at Fairfield University. She resides with her husband, two children, and ten cats in southwestern Connecticut.

To connect with Tiffany

LinkedIn: Tiffany-Donovan-Green

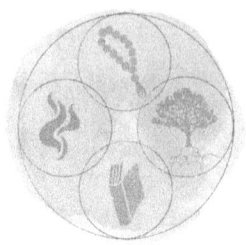

YOU CAME OUTTA YOUR MOMMA'S BUTT

Jeanie Griffin

I had the most wonderful day with my four and three-quarters granddaughter the other day. She is quite a conversationalist, so we discussed many topics, including why her mother had stitches when her older twin brothers were born but no stitches were required when she was born. As she explained it, "Momma did not need stitches because I came outta Momma's butt." Earlier that year, she and her brothers had the opportunity to play on a farm where they gathered eggs from the free-range chickens. One of her brothers held an egg triumphantly above his head and exclaimed he gathered the fresh chicken egg "right out of the chicken's butt." I guess his experience explained no stitches needed by her own birth. I did not follow up to clarify. Some things are better left up to the parents.

Later she was sitting on a brick wall outside savoring a peanut butter and jelly sandwich as she expressed sounds of enjoyment. She looked up at me with eyes sparking and said, "You know what I love more than a peanut butter and jelly sandwich?" "No," I replied. "Just a jelly sandwich!" she squealed, and we both laughed.

I have had the blessed and mesmerizing experience of living

92

close and watching her and her twin brothers grow since shortly after their births. Grandchildren are so very special. It is so easy to see the purity, joy, awe, kindness, wisdom, sweetness in children, and I want my grands to see how perfect, whole, and complete they are.

It was difficult for me to see my inherent goodness until much later in my life. It was then I learned life was about waking up to my True Self. They will learn that, too, but I must admit I want to wrap my grandchildren in a bubble so they never experience the slings and arrows we all do. Kahlil Gibran stated in his book, *The Prophet*, "Your pain is the breaking of the shell that encloses your understanding."[1] I wrote that quote in my journal when I was fifteen.

I am told I was an energetic, sweet, funny, and delightful child. My younger self went through some really hard times. Between ages fifteen and twenty-one, both my parents died. In response to the pain of those deaths, I became self-reliant and filled with resentment toward God and life in general. I have since learned to take care of and appreciate my younger self, but for years I dragged her through resentment. Today, I know the sacred child I am guided me on my spiritual path where she taught me two spiritual truths that still guide my life today:

1. **My True Self is an "Original Recipe," a Unique Energetic Spiritual Vibration created out of an Invisible Power, some call God, Spirit, or Creator.**

2. **I am loved, protected, and guided by that Invisible Power, which, when sought, will reveal Itself to me in a way that I understand, so Its light can shine through me.**

These two Truths are not unique to me. They are true for you, the reader, as well, so I will share what my younger self taught me.

Spiritual Truth #1: My True Self is an "Original Recipe," a Unique Energetic Spiritual . . . Vibration created out of an Invisible Power some call God, Spirit or Creator

I originated in the mind of the Infinite and was released as a Unique Energetic Spiritual Vibration of energy and light. My unique vibration, which I call my Original Recipe or True Self, is one of love, peace, kindness, joy, creativity, beauty, curiosity, light, abundance, expansiveness, and so much more. No one is exactly like me. I am unique. I may look like one or both of my parents, siblings, or other relatives, but that is simply a result of DNA while I use a body on Earth. Before I incarnated into the body that emerged from the DNA of my parents, I was a Unique Energetic Spiritual Vibration, an Original Recipe within the Oneness of the Creator. Now if all that sounds too woo-woo, just watch any child between birth and four years old and you will see purity, energy, light, and a dozen more beautiful qualities. We all are emanations of the God Light and therefore perfect, whole, and complete. We just don't always look that way to ourselves or to others.

When a child forms in the womb of the mother, the Unique Energetic Spiritual Vibration or Original Recipe takes on human form. We eat through a tube, we do not breathe air, and we float around in fluid. Our spiritual identity does not ever change because it is made of energy and energy never dies. Only our form changes. When we are finished using this body, it will disintegrate or dematerialize, and our Original Recipe will transition into another form or perhaps go back into the Oneness of the Creator.

Initially, I had trouble understanding what she meant by "Original Recipe", so my younger self explained it another way. "Think of water with a molecular makeup of H_2O," she said. "If we put water in the freezer, it takes on the form of ice, but its original recipe is H_2O. If we leave it on the counter, it changes form again to look like water, but its original recipe is still H_2O.

It changes form again when it evaporates into a gas, but it is still H_2O. The point is the original recipe never changes. The same is true for all creations."

She went on to give the example of a rose or oak tree. Just as a rose or an oak tree is the final product, when planted, it does not look like the beautiful rose or the huge oak tree. Each begins as an acorn or small plant, and ultimately, if the environment is supportive, they grow into a recognizable rose or oak tree. If we look at a tree and do not know what kind it is, we will only learn its true nature by the fruit it bears. The fruit is an outward expression of its inward nature. The Invisible Creator within emerges to show the Original Recipe. Even though there are hundreds of roses, oak trees or fruit trees, each is unique. The Creator does not replicate. It Shines Its light uniquely through every Original Recipe.

We are born with everything we need to be the unique expression of our Original Recipe also called our True Self.

As children, we are so pure and perfect, but we are born into this world that vibrates at a lower speed than the Creator, so we go through what she called "Birth Amnesia". As we grow, we attempt to navigate through this lower vibration on Earth. Our focus becomes one of survival in the world around us. Everything we do is to make ourselves safe. We react to things outside ourselves. Our focus is on the outside world and how to operate within it. We live from a limited self and focus on what is seen and known. It is a life of survival, self-reliance, and essentially reactive fear. The farther we dive into that lower vibration of negativity and fear, the more we become separated from our True Self. We live in the world of appearances where our compulsions and fears become our solutions. At some point, our solutions or plans for life do not work so we finally surrender, admitting we are FRESH OUTTA PLANS® and need new direction. I arrived at that point after years of self-reliance and resentment.

I had to stop and take a deep dive into introspection and

self-examination. I asked myself, "What am I afraid of? Why am I so unhappy? What is keeping me stuck?" I uncovered old ideas in my thinking that placed me in positions to be hurt. Lies I told myself hardened into laws or rules that keep me in bondage. The lies most often were about separation, loss, lack, limitation, fear of death, unworthiness, scarcity, oppression, guilt, or shame to name a few. I was not living from my Original Recipe made of love, joy, peace, generosity, kindness, abundance, creativity, beauty, symmetry, harmony, well-being, and community. I wanted something different, but what? How?

Spiritual Truth #2: I am loved, protected, and guided by an Invisible Power that, when sought, will reveal Itself to me in a way that makes sense to me, so It can shine Its light through me.

What I know today that I forgot through birth amnesia is that the Oneness, the Creator God, is always broadcasting. Children know how to communicate with the Creator but we slowly forget how to listen to your intuition. We are not encouraged how to pay attention to the external or internal hints nudging us. We are taught to follow adults. We are not taught that our first and original form of communication in the energetic or vibrational world is revelation and that revelation as a form of communication still exists. Because revelation leaves a *knowing* inside rather than a verbal explanation, it makes discussing this matter more complicated because of the limitations of words. Understanding revelation communication also required perception to change from believing that the world of phenomena and appearances is reality, to the Truth of living from the mystery of life. This change in perception means living from the intangible where it does not always make sense and to where appearances are not real. It takes using spiritual practices to raise our vibration until our consciousness remembers how we were attached to the Creator. We do not need to FIND a spiritual connection. We must REMEMBER our original connection to the Creator.

My FRESH OUTTA PLANS® program described on my website, https://www.freshouttaplans.com, provides a method for reconnecting with the Creator's Oneness, reconnecting with our own Original Recipe and reconnecting to others.

Before we can put spiritual practices into place, we must first identify ways in which we get mired down by the vibration of negativity. As humans, we focus on survival and, therefore, we developed defense mechanisms, old ideas, and other solutions that kept us safe. It is as if in the delivery room we were issued an invisible backpack survival kit. As we experienced life on life's terms, we tried solutions in each situation. If the solution appeared to solve the problem or improve the situation, we added it to our backpack titled Plans for Life. For instance, as an infant we have no language, no clue who anyone is, but we instinctively know how to get our needs met. We cry. Others come running to feed us and give us a clean diaper. Aha! We discover crying gets me a dry diaper and a full tummy. Crying works and I am safe. So . . . crying goes into the Plans for Life backpack.

This operant conditioning, as psychologists refer to it, does not stop in infancy. We continue to learn through rewards and punishments into adulthood, and we continue to add many solutions to our Plans for Life backpack. Any time we are faced with a problem, we reach into our backpack and grab a solution. "Not a problem," we say. "I know just what I can use on *it*." We look into our backpack for the perfect plan to use on *it*. Some people face the same *it,* but they use different plans. Let's say, the *it* they faced is divorce. One person's plan might be to drink too much or to smoke pot while another's plan might be to work harder or move to another town. The important thing to remember is that each person believes the plan used is a solution. Sometimes the plan used appears to some people to be a problem. When an alcoholic is told their drinking is a problem, it makes no sense to the drinker because drinking is their solution or plan.

Sometimes the plan is rewarded by our society even if it hurts the person. The person whose plan it is to work harder might get Citizen of the Year but might die early of a heart attack because of job stress. The person whose plan is to depend only on themselves because they do not trust other people might hide the fact that they are very lonely.

When the backpack finally gets too heavy and one is brave enough to ask, "What am I afraid of? Why am I so unhappy? What is keeping me stuck?" then that person might be ready for introspection and self-examination. During the Untangle the Mind module of the FRESH OUTTA PLANS® program, one will take off that backpack and throw it on the floor where all the solutions can be sorted through to see which ones are working and which ones are keeping the person stuck. One can also examine the beliefs or lies you are telling yourself that have hardened into laws that keep you in bondage. Each of us must become very familiar with the laws in our thinking so we can change them and not become bound by them.

In the Untangle the Mind module, we examine the negativity of fear, lack, loss, separation, scarcity, limitation, resentment, unworthiness, oppression, and more. In the Experience the Invisible module, we review and explore our spiritual beliefs and build spiritual practices that assist with raising individual vibrations and experiences.

So how do we raise our vibration? We learn spiritual practices such as affirmative prayer, meditation, visioning, affirmation cards, seeing with new eyes, and hearing with new ears. We look past appearances to infinite possibilities and ever-expanding good. We let go of worldly ego identities and begin to identify as our True Selves, coming back to remember we are the Light of the World, at one with the Most-High. Our Heart Light is our Original Recipe.

We never go through this process alone because in the Connect with Community module, we work together for support and, more importantly, we also focus on being of service to each other and the greater global community. Joy, peace, love, abundance, generosity, kindness, creativity, well-being, beauty doesn't come from the world; it comes from the Creator shining Its Light in, as, and through your Original Recipe. You are the face of the Creator that showed up as you. You are the Creator's energy that changes form but never dies.

My younger self connected me with myself so I could know my Original Recipe and live my purpose. She connected me with the mystery of my Creator so I could know IT. She connected me with a tribe of people I call "God with Skin On" who support my spiritual journey. Because of my connection to self, God, and others, I can be of service to others. So can you.

The world we desire comes through individuals, as each of us shows the world our light inside. We are the fish we gotta catch. We can create a world of higher vibration where we are always becoming more of ourselves, but first we must wake up to our true nature. We can live from the mystery of life. In other words, the pair of glasses you have been rummaging around trying to find are sitting on top of your head. Stop thinking, judging, and trusting appearances. Find a tribe of seekers. Ask. Seek. Knock. Come raise your vibration and your consciousness will rise above appearances. Reveal the invisible inside you, just like the rose or the oak tree. Reveal your True Self so the world can see the God Light shine in, as, and through you. Be the Original Recipe the Creator made. You do not have to know how. You simply have to be willing to surrender and admit you are FRESH OUTTA PLANS®. Next, ask for guidance from your intuition, the Creator and others living life from their Original Recipes.

1—Kahlil Gibran, The Prophet (New York City, NY: Alfred A. Knopf, 1923)

ABOUT JEANIE GRIFFIN

Jeanie Griffin is a #1 international best-selling author, keynote speaker, VIP retreat leader, shamanic practitioner, mental health counselor, and addictions trauma psychotherapist. She is the founder and CEO of the Los Angeles business FRESH OUTTA PLANS®. She holds a master's degree and is professionally licensed in California and Texas.

Her virtual sessions and online courses help people with spiritual questions, challenging relationships, codependency, substance abuse challenges, anxiety, and depression. She has the right combination of compassion, humor, and honesty. See her website for products for sale and services offered.

Jeanie Griffin has appeared on *Divorce Talk* with Dr. Sue, *Where All Things Are Possible* with Kate Butler, *Everybody* with Dr. Angela Sadler Williamson, *The Relaxed Dog* with Robert Ober, and *We're All Psychic* with Lisa Rusczyk.

She is an assistant producer of *Authentic Conversations: Deep Talk with the Masters*, a documentary written, directed, and produced by Dr. Angela Sadler Williamson featuring Jack Canfield, Patty Aubery, and Kate Butler. It is the first in a series of documentaries about the importance of having authentic conversations.

To connect with Jeanie

https://www.freshouttaplans.com
Facebook Group: FRESH OUTTA PLANS® Community Group and FRESH OUTTA PLANS®
TikTok: @freshouttaplans
Instagram: @jeaniegriffinla and @freshouttaplans
Podcast: *The Recovered Therapist* with Jeanie Griffin
Amazon Books: *Women Who Rise* by Jeanie Griffin
Leading with Legacy Kate Butler Editor
Summary: https://linktr.ee/freshouttaplans

JUST BE

Christina Macro

I arrived at the Cape Cod Hospital early in the morning after driving through the night at Mach speeds, not even caring whether I would be pulled over, with only one focus: to hug my mom and ultimately pack her shit and move her in with me as soon as she was discharged from the hospital. I had just renovated the recreation room in my townhouse to accommodate my mom's arrival for her winter stays with me. We had just worked through the complications of preparing her home for sale. I had just finished doing everything possible to ensure she could sell the home, take the proceeds, and live her remaining years without financial stress or worry. We had entered that phase of life where the tables had turned. I was planning to take care of this woman until she left the world. With joy. For me, it was a way to thank her for the sacrifices she made in her lifetime; those sacrifices were never all that clear to me until now. But now I knew.

I don't know what I thought I would face when I entered her hospital room that day. But I wasn't prepared. I took one look at my mom and turned my head away from her because I did not want her to see me cry at what I saw. "Am I in the right room? Lee Silva?" The nurse nodded her head. "That is *not* my mother . . . She looks nothing like the beautiful, stunning, confident woman that I had always known as my mother." Again, the nurse nodded, this time saying my mother had "been through a lot overnight." Finally accepting the nurse's confirmations, I wiped my tears, took a deep breath, pasted on a smile, turned to my mother, and opened my arms in an expression of love otherwise reserved for moms greeting their school-age children after a perfect dance recital or school science fair project win.

I spent the entire day with Mom, reading magazines, sharing stories, confirming that I had done what was needed in order to sell her home, hugging her, and assuring her that I loved her so much, while never letting go of her swollen hands.

That night, I went to the cafeteria for dinner and came back to a horrific and tragic scene unfolding. Her breathing was failing her again. She was awake, gasping for air even with an oxygen mask forcing pure oxygen into her lungs to support her healing. I grabbed both of her hands in mine, stood over her bed, looking straight into her beautiful soul through her kind and soft eyes, and said, "Relax, breathe with me . . . in and out . . . in and out. I am not letting you go, Mom. I am not letting you go, I'll never let you go. Just breathe with me."

I will never shake the excruciating moment when I looked into her eyes that night. She looked at me with sheer terror and fear. A look that I had never once seen in this woman. This spirited, kind, and calm woman was suddenly speaking directly to my soul through the look in her eyes. Without words, she begged me for help. She begged me tearfully and painfully to help. I pressed the nurses station call button. I pressed it like a Jeopardy contestant trying to ring in over the faster opponent. In a moment's notice, ICU nurses rushed in, calm and steady, to stabilize my mother. I stood there helpless and afraid. I grappled in complete distress over what I could not do for her. I felt weak and defenseless in my promise to never let her go. I was asked to leave the room while the nurses tended to my mom.

I was dazed. I walked the halls of the Cape Cod Hospital that night. I got to the maternity ward. I saw the babies through the glass and thought about myself being a newborn in this very same hospital while my mom and dad rested in a room down the hall, waiting to bring their almost-Christmas baby home. I walked through the ER where I had come as a child when I broke both of my wrists on the playground in elementary school. I recollected moments of my life in which I was the patient while my mother sat worried in a waiting room. I also recalled moments of my life when I, as a parent, brought my own son to the ER. I wandered aimlessly to the hospital main entrance that night and watched as people drifted in and out looking confused, distracted, concerned, sad, while others were happy and relieved.

I eventually walked out the front door and down the street to the edge of the ocean to watch the ferries float in and out of Lewis Bay. I sat on a swing and cried watching the sun set—a metaphor for what I was experiencing back at the hospital. I cried for a life that hung in the balance. I cried for my own self-worth. I cried for not knowing. I cried for knowing. I cried for the years that passed and the time I had spent not cherishing each moment in joy and living each day realizing that my time here was always limited. I cried for my total ignorance of the fact that the amount of time we each have should not only affect how we create the rules but how we live our truths unabashedly and without abandon.

It was a hard goodbye. I was oblivious to the permanence of it. While the nurses pulled out the tubes and turned off the machines the next day, she once again opened her eyes and looked at me. I saw into her soul again, but this time through eyes at peace, resolved in knowing it was her time. I held her swollen hands. I bent over and whispered, "I love you, Mom. It's okay. I promise to take care of everything. I'm never leaving you."

Within minutes, she was gone. A shell lying on a hospital bed with no life left to give. Her strength and confidence were now absent. Her energy vanished in a moment. While I sat dazed and confused as those same hospital visitors I had observed wandering in and out of the hospital entrance the night before, I shifted to gratitude. After all, how many people have the opportunity to sit by their mother's death bed, hold her hands, tell her how much they love her, and say goodbye? I know she heard me. I know she left this world knowing, without question, that I was there for her. This gift of knowing was greater than any single gift in the world.

Many years before, I woke up and knew it was a beautiful day for my first girls trip with my mom to Antigua—as it was every day in the Caribbean. I sat under the short hut with my mom. That day on the beach, we connected in a way that I had never experienced before. I remember asking her if she had any regrets in life. And the floodgates opened. She mentioned things like growing old, being married to my dad, and her five failed marriages after that, never knowing love, never knowing the life she desired, the shame of her childhood, the bitterness she had with her own mother, the disconnectedness of her siblings, never even knowing her childhood dreams let alone living out those dreams, feeling like she had to grow up before she was ready, the fun and adventure of growing up in Provincetown, the love she had for her father, and on and on she went. I sat stunned listening to her share intimate details about her life and how she dealt with the disappointments at every age and every stage.

That night, I wrote her a letter as if I were a wise sage looking from the outside in but with a youthful perspective on her life; I aligned my own experiences with hers and how I handled them on my own. My letter was never sent to her, but it became an ongoing writing prompt for the journal of my life and how the lessons of her life became the gratitudes of mine.

I embarked on a journey to become the best version of myself after hearing of the regrets of my own mother. My love letter to my mom became the foundation of everything beautiful that happened after she died and a writing prompt for me to pay honor to her as she rests peacefully forever.

What is the meaning and richness of life? It is knowing that there will always be regret—but also accepting that those regrets, in a most hurtful and painful way, can produce a way forward on the path toward significance.

If I could have gotten through to her even only one message, it would have been for her to deeply appreciate and honor the privilege of simply being alive. She never knew gratitude or pure joy for that matter. For her, gratitude and joy were experiences *given to* her not experienced *through* her.

What I mostly wanted to say to my mom was "Focus on who you are and be more of that." Who she was was always enough. She never could see that. *Just be.*

This mantra got me through many tumultuous years in my life: when I found myself raising my son alone, when I lived in my car while attempting to work and feed my child, when I uprooted his life for the opportunities in DC, when I got married to an abusive and unkind man, when I got up every morning and prayed for mercy. I would remind myself relentlessly to *just be.* Allowing myself the grace to step forward each and every single day into a better version of myself meant truly that each daisy chain of moments would add up to a life of love and grace.

For my mom, there was this longing for something she believed that she just could not have or experience. The human shell she lived in was this tall, stunningly beautiful, strong, stoic, kind, quiet, charming, empathetic woman who was outwardly accepting while inwardly agitated at not ever getting what she longed for: love and acceptance. I just don't think she knew that love and acceptance was actually within herself. My mother longed to be something that was always an arm's length from her grasp. She never knew that she had the power to reach those dreams were it not for the thick armor of fear that jailed her emotions and zest within her body. She never believed in herself.

This message would have led her to truly embrace the fact that her life could have been so much more meaningful if she could have focused on self-reflection and gratitude. I just don't think anyone taught her that she was not powerless to achieving fulfillment in her life. She brought a level of uniqueness and joy that was authentic and overwhelmingly delightful to those who knew her. In her final years, I watched her desperately seek to find connection in a world of silence.

After my mom died, I found a handful of disposable cameras in her nightstand. I gathered them, with a few other important belongings during the clean-out of my childhood home. It was over a year later that I mustered the courage to drop off those cameras and get the film developed. I received the films back and sat quietly in my bedroom flipping one image after the other. Every single photo was of me. Sitting on the beach reading, sitting at a distance at the hotel we stayed in, smiling at people we met along the way, drinking water on a cruise ship in Greece. All photos of me. As if she were this personal paparazzi and was documenting my life whenever we traveled together. The images were haunting. When I flipped through each one, I saw myself as only my mother saw me: her greatest accomplishment and her most treasured art. These images broke me, not because I didn't see the beauty in who I am but because I was blatantly unaware of the sadness in the part of her soul that those images represented— who she wanted to become. Who she never had the courage to become. And what I represented to her. A version of herself that she had only ever dreamed possible. What she didn't know was it was her strength, her armor, her inner beauty, and her inability to grasp the love that she so deserved that drove me to my own passions. I was a reflection of her soul. And that reflection was most evident in those photos. Those photos were a reflection of her belief that she was never enough.

My mom knew when it was her time. I have experienced this in my life not only with her but most recently with an ex-boyfriend. He called me the very night he died to tell me how much he loved and trusted me and that he told his mother all about me. He asked me if it was okay that he told his mom about me; she was sitting right next to him at the time. He regaled on and on about our twenty-year relationship turned platonic friendship and told his mom over and over that I was his soulmate and he loved me more than anything. I wasn't sure if he was okay because my ex-boyfriend never really expressed his feelings to me, not like that anyway.

The point is people know when they are leaving. They tell us loud and clear in statements they make, in passing comments, in a quiet declaration, or in baring their soul right before they fall asleep peacefully forever on their living room couch next to their own mom. My mom knew too. It was mid-June, and I was working hard at unraveling the intricacies of selling her home. There were so many legalities that I had to unwind and clear up for her, but being an experienced twenty-year real estate broker meant that I could navigate all of it with her best interests at heart. During one particular phone call, my mom made it clear that she wanted to sell the home and live off the proceeds, and when she died, she wanted me and my brother to split whatever was left. When I discussed her options, she said, "Thank you, baby girl." *Huh?* My mom never called me "baby girl." It felt sweet but odd all at the same time. You know, the quiet declaration: *I'm leaving you soon, please pay attention to these cryptic messages.*

Not soon after, I mentioned coming home for Fourth of July weekend. I put in for time off at work, but my boss denied my request. I called my mom to tell her that my boss would not give me the time off. I could hear the sadness in her tone. She had never sounded disappointed before. She was telling me it was time. I just didn't listen.

My mother never ever learned to find her voice and speak up. She never made it clear when she was hurting. She never expressed it when she wanted something from others. She just shrugged her shoulders and called it a day. That day was no different. I inherited some of those qualities from my mom. I just never wanted to feel like a burden to others. I never wanted to be the complainer, the negative one, the one making demands. So I knew that she was pushing me to get home; I just couldn't do it that particular weekend. And if I could go back in time, I would have made it home far more often. I would have found my own voice to speak my truth to my asshole ex-boss, and I would have screamed, "No, douchebag, my family and my mother are more important than a job or presentation, so you can just fuck right off with your denial of a day off today!" But I didn't. Because I learned to squelch my own voice from the model and example of my mother. I know that if my mother knew the meaning she held in my life, she would have demanded that I stand up for myself and set the boundary and not betray myself.

If I could have one last conversation with my mom, I would have made sure she knew, without a doubt, that she never knew the depth of significance she held in my life. Perhaps I was not the husband she always dreamed of, the career that she desired, the contentment that comes with wealth, the lifestyle she dreamed of, the family that she wished for, or the adventures that she longed to experience. But I was her daughter. Her daughter that loved her deeply and without conditions. The person who saw her through the same lens of those disposable cameras—a perfect human who loved only as she knew how.

And that love *was* enough. *She* was enough. And life did love her back—but in ways that she never recognized as meaningful and passionate. And now it is too late to tell her.

ABOUT CHRISTINA MACRO

Christina is a genuine leader, an intellectual, an authentic entrepreneur tapping into her own inspiration to lead others to greatness. As a servant leader, she has succeeded exponentially in her career in real estate as a Residential and Commercial Broker but also personally as a mentor, coach, mother, and friend. Through humor and compassion, she shares her stories in hopes that others discover ways to find and use their voices to dig deep to the core of their being to radiate from the inside out. Christina truly believes that beauty emanates from our souls and we have the ability to build dreams from a centered space using self-respect and self-awareness as the footing. We are all on this planet to support one another, and Christina inherently lives through her generosity of spirit, which is unmatched in guiding others to excellence.

To connect with Christina

Facebook: Christina Macro
Instagram: @thebrainybroker
Twitter: @thebrainybroker
LinkedIn: Christina Macro

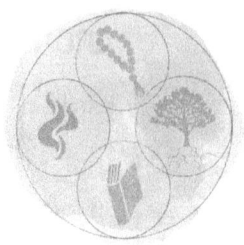

YOU ARE GOOD ENOUGH

Melissa Malland

As I am getting ready to begin my junior year of high school, I stare in the mirror. I do not see a vision of myself in the mirror. As I peer intently into the mirror, my visions are of all the pretty and attractive girls I pass in the hallway who I desperately want to look like. I would notice the long, silky, bouncy hair as one girl would saunter by and think about how I was walking around with a frizzy mop on my head. *Why can't I have that hair?* How about the girl with the perfect teeth and smile while I was supporting these hideous "clear" braces at the time? Then there were the girls who had the most stylish, up-to-date outfits that never seemed to repeat. Each day their clothing would look better than the previous day. Next would be the girl with the perfect body, the athletic one, or the highly intelligent girl. Or worse yet, the girl that had ALL OF THE ABOVE. The guys in school were drawn to these girls—where someone like me wasn't in the crosshairs. I might as well have been invisible.

Looking in the mirror became worse on a daily basis, and my self-image began to crumble to pieces. I was giving up my power and self-worth to other people. If a guy I was interested in didn't seem interested in me or I wasn't sought out by a guy, the letdown was immeasurable. I was convinced it was because I wasn't pretty, athletic, well-dressed, smart, or all of the above. All of my friends (or so it seemed) had a boyfriend. The words and phrases I would say to myself on a daily basis were things I wouldn't even say to an enemy. I became my own worst enemy and my biggest critic. My mother had caught on to my insecurity issues and would write me notes to read before I left for school in the morning to help boost my self-esteem. I became so accustomed to the daily struggles and pain that it just became part of me.

My high school career that should have been filled with joy and new experiences was clouded by extreme sadness and despair from such poor self-image. I prayed for better days and happiness, looking for some silver lining from the dark clouds, that I, myself, was creating.

I didn't know that at the time. I was searching in all the wrong places for the right answer, and it would take me a very long time to figure that out.

I decided to take a job on the boardwalk at the Jersey Shore in Seaside Heights, New Jersey. During that time period, Seaside Heights was a very busy tourist destination with much for the tourist to do, such as the boardwalk, arcades, the beach, water parks, and many places to satisfy your hunger for pizza, ice cream, boardwalk fries, and more. Keep in mind that this was a place where many locals of the nearby towns would get summer jobs. This was the place to work, earn some money, meet new people, and catch up with your friends from school. It was the best of both worlds.

I remember my best friend and I got a job at the same place. We were stoked because we would work the same days and hours. The only difference was that I worked at the arcade and she worked at the store. That meant we could spend time together during our lunch breaks. It was summer, the weather was warm, and people were genuinely in a good mood. I began meeting a lot of people, both female and male. I was a social person who loved to have deep, meaningful conversations—and not just about the weather. As an educator, I am and will always be a lifelong learner, so when I socialize, I enjoy learning about and from other people. I found out that forming relationships with my new coworkers was not only boosting my mood but also my self-esteem. That is where I met my first "real" boyfriend and had my first real relationship.

Ironically enough, I was hesitant to date him despite his attempts, and it took almost two months before I finally accepted being his girlfriend. Now my self-esteem was soaring, for all the wrong reasons, I may add; however, it was sure invigorating to have someone doting over you. Those insecurities only took a short time period off before they came back with a vengeance. We went to two different schools. He went to a private school, and I went to a public school across town. It was when he showed me his yearbook and I saw his beautiful classmates that the self-doubt and insecurities trickled right back into my mind, wreaking havoc.

I was seeking things from the wrong people and situations. The real me was hidden behind all of this self-doubt. I wore a mask and feared having my true colors shine from within. It took me a very long time to realize what I was doing wrong. It became worse when the relationship ended, and there I was again blaming myself for all my flaws while comparing myself to the girls he'd go to school with every day.

Half of my high school experience was shrouded by my self-critic, the worst critic of all, and stealing my everyday joy. It inhibited my growth, made me question myself, and had stolen my self-confidence. I remember always walking in a room full of people, beyond nervous and riddled with anxiety, wondering if I was good enough. The negative self-talk was suffocating me, and it felt like I was just being pulled down in quicksand.

Dear younger self, stop seeking validation from others and believe in yourself. Please do not rely on others to make you happy; it is a self-fulfilling necessity, and only you can make that happen. When it comes to a romantic relationship, continue to realize your worth, and do not become too dependent on that person—as if you can't live without them. Don't lose who you are as a person when you become involved in a romantic relationship. Your partner should enhance who you are as a person, support your goals, and allow you to still have your own life outside of your relationship with them.

Oh, my younger self, please stop feeling like you need someone to make you whole. The authentic people in your life will love you for who you are no matter what. You can make your dreams come true, and please stop obsessing and dwelling in the past wondering why. Let go of the past, live in the moment, and stop giving everyone else in your life power over you, power over what you do, where you go, your interests, and who you are authentically.

Younger self, stop fearing what others think, stop overthinking, it's inhibiting your growth, robbing you of the present, which we all know is a gift, and stealing your peace, sanity, and joy from living your life to the fullest. You can't control what's going to happen, younger self. I have realized that I spent the majority of my forty-six years on this Earth second-guessing, overthinking, full of anxiety and self-doubt, which were contributing factors to my sadness. It has stolen my life. Please don't make this mistake. Live for today. We don't hold the crystal ball for the future, yet I've spent so much time worrying about it.

Younger self, enjoy living in the moment, forget the past, and if there is someone who chooses to leave your life, let them go. Does it hurt? Yes, it hurts. Allow yourself some time to grieve, but don't let it keep you down. Keep moving along. It is okay to be alone.

Younger self, I was always so petrified to be alone and placed so much emphasis on being alone that I never enjoyed my own company. Please don't mistake this for me advising you to not socialize with others, especially since you are a social person. Just don't be with a partner for the sake of not being alone. The right authentic people will love you for who you are on the inside and outside. Worrying isn't going to stop anything that we can't control. I'll quote what a good friend had said to me: "Don't worry about me, I'll always be okay." I sat back and thought, *That is the motto I need to instill in my life.* Younger self, growing up, I never thought I was good enough. I never thought I'd be okay without a boyfriend. I never thought I'd be okay without a husband. And now as a mother, as my kids get older, I think, *Will I be okay when they are out on their own?* YES . . . I will be okay for so many reasons. It took a long time to get here, but my confidence is solid. If something were to happen in my marriage, of course it would be sad, but I finally feel like I would be okay. I am my own most valuable asset, and just because we go through different phases in life, some being very unpleasant, it doesn't mean my life has to stop. It doesn't mean I can't do all the things I want to do and that I have to depend on a partner to do those things. It is okay to be me and show it to others, and it is okay if I am alone in doing so.

Younger self, practice this now, speak up, show them the funny, authentic person that you are, the quirky person, the naïve person, and the flawed person. Stop worrying if you said the wrong thing or had a bad hair day. These things do not define you. You don't need others to make you feel valuable; feel it within yourself! Compliments are great, but *don't* hang on them. Don't obsess over what a potential partner has said to you. Yes, it is heart-warming and endearing, along with being genuine. But say to yourself, "That is awesome that they see me the way I see myself," and then move right along! Younger self, don't hang onto everyone's words, pleasant or unpleasant. Do not hold onto others' words, criticisms, or compliments. They do not fulfill you; you fulfill yourself. Throw away the negative self-talk and self-doubt along with thinking you don't fit in and let your true soul shine.

My fears of insecurity ended up coming true with fidelity issues, so I wasted time worrying most of my life about what I couldn't control anyway. Younger self, please realize that if sometimes relationships don't work out, regardless of if it's a friendship or a romantic relationship, stop beating yourself up. Take your power back, dust yourself off, and move on.

Younger self, walk into a room with your held head high and don't worry who is sitting with who or how you look. Don't be afraid to sit alone. Your energy will attract the people meant to be in your life.

Younger self, it took me almost thirty years to realize and recognize who I am and my worth. Now I walk into a room, and I don't wonder if I am good enough for other people, I wonder if those people are good enough for me. Dearest younger self, do not bury the beauty within. Let it resonate with grace and humility while you exude confidence.

ABOUT MELISSA MALLAND

Melissa is a #1 international best-selling author for *Women Who Shine* and *Women Who Dream*. After suffering from postpartum depression and from anxiety her whole life, Melissa Malland is a passionate advocate for depression and anxiety, along with all other types of mental illness. She is a mom of three young men, ages twenty, seventeen, and fourteen.

Despite being passionate about her own children, her husband of twenty-one years, and mental illness, Melissa's other passion is teaching. Melissa is a sixth-grade language arts teacher at the middle school level. She has been an inspiration to all her past and present students. She has been embracing being a middle school teacher for twenty-three years. Melissa holds a teaching license along with her principal licensure for the state of NJ. Melissa has an associate's degree in liberal arts, a bachelor of arts, and a master's degree in education administration.

She has impacted thousands of young minds during her career where her students have become more like family. Melissa brings her advocacy on mental health into her classroom. It was imperative for her to focus on mental health with her students to assist with the issues that arose within education during the pandemic. Melissa plans to continue embracing tomorrow's youth by teaching her students to find their voice and encourage self-care and growth. Finally, Melissa hopes to begin her motivational speaking career in the near future.

To connect with Melissa

myboyz326@yahoo.com
Facebook: Mals Meliss
Instagram: @Missy_gm
Twitter: @MelissaMalland3

DON'T STEP ON THE DISH TOWEL

Erin McCahill

When the cool crisp air hits and the smell of fresh-cut Christmas trees is in the air, those twinkling lights talk to my soul and bring me back to when we were three years old. After all these years, we still giggle and look for the magic of the season in every moment and believe and dream of all the possibilities out there. But after the season is over, some of the magic goes away. You leave me, you go silent even though I know you are there. And some years, you stay still and quiet, nowhere to be found.

"Oh, I am always here with you. Where do you think I go?"

I don't know. These past few years really have made me more curious than ever where you go. It has made me realize how incredible our journey is. I wish I could have told you beforehand all life had in store for you. That way I could have prepared you better for the incredible, the not so incredible, and everything in between that you would encounter. Life is never going to be easy. I mean, how fun would that be?

"*Easy*? That is not in our vocabulary, and you know that!"

"Stop fooling yourself, it is part of who we are and it made us who we are today. Be proud! You have accomplished so much and there is so much more to come. Have we ever had it easy? Think about it, Erin, tell me what is the earliest memory you have of us having it easy? Tell me!"

You are right, we really haven't.

Do you remember we were three years old, so excited for the holiday season, dressed in our winter coat, our favorite saddle shoes, and hair of course in pigtails and bows? We were walking through the dark, cold, crisp night on the wide-open black top toward the twinkling lights to get our Christmas tree? We were laughing with huge smiles as Mom and Dad held our hands and swung us in the air every few steps.

Then . . .

We didn't see it coming from a mile away. We didn't know life was going to change when you ran ahead and stepped on the dish towel.

"Wait a minute. Not me. *We* stepped on that towel that was lying on the ground. I remember what it looked like. Do you?"

How could I ever forget? It was an orange, white, brown plaid dish towel lying perfectly flat on the ground. You decided to walk ahead of Mom and Dad, and down you went.

"No, *we* decided to walk on the towel together, and down *we* went right into that covered-up black hole."

It is clear as that evening's perfect star-filled sky. It hurt. We were in tears not knowing what happened, Mom screaming and the tree lot workers running toward us, Dad pulling us up. Across from the tree lot, there was a lone building that just happened to have a dentist office, and it was open. We sat in that dentist chair as he fixed us up and told us we lost our front teeth. Dad said, "I guess you can ask Santa for your two front teeth," and everyone laughing. Not understanding the meaning and why everyone was laughing, we just went with it, and we had a big smile and were focused, confident, and fearless—ready to get right back out there and get our tree!

"I do remember!"

I look back. You were so confident, sassy, and ready to take on the world after that. Going through photos this year after mom's passing, one keeps showing up: you are standing there posing for the photographer in your white faux-leather-and-fur jacket, patent leather boots, stylish hair, and the biggest toothless smile! Oh, how I wish I had that three-year-old confidence you had.

This was such a pivotal moment in our journey. We were teased and laughed at because we were missing our front teeth all the way through grade school. But you never backed down. You were always strong and confident; you didn't care what people thought of you. You were proud to tell everyone you were wishing for your two front teeth for Christmas this year, *again*. You stood behind what you believed; it amazes me how confident you were. I lost this somehow along the way.

"Why do you think that is? I have always been here, and I have never left. I watch you today with more intelligence, more sophistication, more life experiences, more to bring to the table, and I am wondering what happened along the way. Why did you lose your confidence, and why don't you feel the way I felt when we lost our front teeth: confident and sassy, ready to conquer the world?"

Wow, that is really perceptive of you!

This is a hard one. I look back, and the last time I remember being fully confident, fearless, never looking back, speaking my mind without worrying what others would think was in the fifth grade. I was interviewed by the local paper on the playground, and they asked:

"Do you think the April school vacation is needed? What do you plan to do this vacation?"

I said, "No, I don't think we need the vacation. We have to finish our SATs and get ready for next year. The weekends are enough. I'm not planning on going anywhere. I like school, plus we just had a vacation in February." I was the only one that said no, the daughter of a high school teacher/coach. There was a lot of chatter around this, but I remained confident and loved my interview and photo in the paper.

From this point on, I allowed outside noise to take this confidence away from me. I let things get to me and gave my self-power away. There are many lessons that would have helped stop the unraveling of my confidence if I had known them then.

Lesson One: Do not listen to the noise around you.

It will tear you down and make you weak. Be strong. Keep an eye on your dreams, the goal line. Be like a racehorse with their blinders, only seeing what is in front of them as they head to the finish line. Always be confident and sassy. Do not give your power away to others; stay in your own confidence unapologetically.

"Wait a minute, Erin! There is another lesson that you have not fully learned. Let's be honest here, your fear of judgment has been holding you back from forging ahead, going after your dreams, and living your life's purpose."

Lesson Two: Do not be fearful of judgment.

"Just like no two snowflakes are alike, no two people are alike. Every person has their special characteristics, and you cannot be like anyone else. So, stand tall, be confident, dream big, let your inner self sparkle—don't let anything get in your way. You will find the 'snowballs' in life that you are supposed to be part of. Don't force it; it won't stay together. The sun will come out and melt it. You are you, you are unique, don't be afraid what others think, be confident."

I get it, but it's hard! People are always telling us what to do, what goal to set, society saying you need to be/look like this, and I'm always trying to be perfect in every aspect to please everyone. It's exhausting and confusing.

"It is. Always helping others first before taking care of yourself, being that people pleaser."

Yes, it is, and I know, we both agree on the next lesson.

Lesson Three: Show up and serve yourself first before you serve others.

You will find your life purpose, and once you do, the universe will shift and bring in an abundance of perfect opportunities to live in the moment and create the life you desire. When you serve others, it will come back and serve you when needed. But you need to show up for yourself first. You need to believe this and live in this manner every day. Not only is it good for others, but it is good for your soul and will direct you to your purpose.

I struggled with this, always listening to others, showing up to serve them first versus taking bits and pieces and showing up for myself before anyone. This caused being taken advantage of in various ways, making wrong decisions, getting stuck, and losing my confidence. Avoid the pain, hurt, disappointment, and anger by putting yourself first and just being you.

Lesson Four: Be vulnerable, ask for help, let others see where you are, listen to your inner self. Just be and go with the flow!

There will be moments that take your breath away. It's okay to be uncomfortable. Ask for help when needed and enjoy those compliments you receive. This is the universe giving back to you that which you have given others. Live in those moments, cherish them; this is when life is aligned. You have this ability to know when the time is right to pay it forward. Do more of this earlier on in life. Never expect anything in return and watch what happens. I always go back to the time I was heartbroken a friend did not show up for a trip. You made sure you enjoyed your time in Disney. At dinner, you saw that couple enjoying every moment of their time together. You were mesmerized, and something inside told you to pay for their dinner. Why them? This is your uniqueness; you have a sense and just know.

Follow that feeling, listen to and watch for the signs. What you did that night was more than you ever expected. We never know what people are going through. You handed the waitress an anonymous note, walked out not waiting for anything in return or to see their reaction. It felt good but what came next was not what you expected. The waitress ran after you and stopped to tell you what you did was so pivotal, inspiring, and kind, she wanted to know all about you, who you were, and your relation to them. When you told her you were just a single girl having dinner, you had no idea who they were, never met them, never saw them until that moment at the restaurant, she was in awe. She had to tell you about them and how incredible your gift was.

That couple was celebrating their final anniversary, as the wife had one wish to celebrate the love of her life where it started before her journey home, which was not too far off. What a beautiful gift you gave them.

"You need to be confident, Erin, in being who you are. You shy away when people do things for you, and you need to get out of this mindset of never letting people see you down.

"It is okay to be you! It's okay to ask for and accept help. It's okay to just be!

"Trust your inner self, that voice, and be confident to chase those goals. Ask for help so you can keep learning like you did as a child. Don't be afraid and don't be ashamed. Don't miss any opportunities because of a lack of confidence. Look at all the instances the universe has given back to you. It has been hard especially this year with all the changes and working through the loss of Mom and finding your new normal. Look at all the friends and how the universe has stepped in to help you through this. It made it easier, didn't it?"

You are right, it did. I just struggle with knowing what to do sometimes and whether I can really do what I want to do.

"Erin, here you go again. It comes down to your confidence. You need to get back to that three-year-old mindset and confidence level. Stop worrying about what others think about you and what they think you should be doing, and you will be on your path to leave an amazing legacy. You don't realize what you accomplished, do you?"

I didn't until I had to slow down this year and realized these lessons would have been helpful earlier on in life.

Lesson Five: Don't rush to grow up. Rush to enjoy every moment in front of you.

I finally heard Dad's message when he left me off at college to live life to your fullest and that these are the best days of your life. Even though he always said this in various ways, it took me until then to finally hear him because I was in a rush to grow up. Which brings me to the next lesson.

Lesson Six: Stop! Take time to fully celebrate your accomplishments.

Being in such a rush to grow up and be the best and please and show others I can do so much, I missed out celebrating all my achievements because I was always looking to what was next. As a highly successful female professional, we sometimes get caught in this race to show we can bring so much more value to the table. But we don't take time to celebrate. We take the fun and celebration out of learning and accomplishing milestone after milestone, and what we don't realize is that this eats away at your confidence when life takes another path, and you start to question your ability and if you are enough.

Lesson Seven: Be more curious; keep making connections! Keep asking questions about everything and everyone before it is too late and you don't have the opportunity to.

I learned this the hard way this year. I knew Mom made a difference in others during her time here but had no idea how impactful she was in so many people's lives until they shared their stories. I learned how confident that four-foot-nine woman was and the legacy she has left behind for me to add to. It makes me sad I was not able to enjoy and celebrate these amazing things with her because I didn't ask, because I was in that rush to grow up. What I did learn is to live a good, purposeful life, giving people hope, inspiring them to be their best and making a difference.

I look at all the lives Mom touched and how many people shared that she made them the person they are today, gave them hope, and helped them live another life. Without her, they would not be where they are today. She was a trailblazer in her time, creating the path for so many in so many ways. Be confident. Life is short; there is not a second chance to do over. Say hi, start a conversation with someone you don't know, invite more people in, don't be afraid, you will be surprised who you might meet and what you will learn.

"But, Erin, do you realize you are leaving a legacy, too? You have inspired others, given them hope, helped them achieve their dreams. Do you realize that?

"No, you don't. Do you?"

Lesson Eight: Do not lose your identity.

"Be confident in what you believe, never let anyone/anything make you feel unworthy, like you need to change your core values instilled in you, that you owe them. Trust what you hear and see."

You are right. The time is now, and I need you to know, though, it has taken years to learn one of the biggest lessons. I am fully committed to and following the next lesson.

Lesson Nine: Listen to the lifeguard (universe).

When that lifeguard starts blowing the whistle and waves the red flag, make sure you do not stay in the shark-infested water. Get out and run. The answers are all being given to you. It is what you do with what you see and hear. Trust yourself. Be confident that the universe is giving you that red flag for a reason.

"It all comes right back to your confidence, Erin. You lost it along the way, but I am here to tell you it is there, and you just need to come grab it. What are you waiting for?"

Never did I realize until now that I lost my confidence. I have been very successful, so I always thought I was confident.

"You are and have been, but not to your full potential."

You are right. I need to get back to that three-year-old, confident, sassy girl ready to take on the world—just being her. We have worked a lot to get to where we are today, but we have some more work to do to get to that three-year-old confidence level. To do this, we need to remember our final lesson.

Lesson Ten: Love yourself, believe in yourself, be proud of your accomplishments, be brave and bold.

There is no perfect or right journey. It is how you react, how you treat yourself. And along the way, make sure you never lose your confidence. I know that I lost my confidence, but I am brave enough and love myself to keep tapping into that three-year-old confidence, share my journey with others to give them hope, and inspire them to take my lessons to never lose their confidence, achieve their dreams, and live their best life. There is so much more to come, and everyday new possibilities show up as I continue to build my confidence and get it all back. Confidence is important, and we are all born with it. We just can't lose it along the way. Losing it makes life messy and a bit harder, but once we get it back, the opportunities that show up are amazing.

I just want to thank you for the confidence that you instilled in me and the lessons I learned on my way back to you. Let's keep working on this journey together and help others along the way.

ABOUT ERIN MCCAHILL

Erin McCahill is a corporate leader, entrepreneur, mentor, innovator, a personal and professional culture creator, and #1 international best-selling author. As a sales and customer experience leader in the telecom, technology, and financial industry, she has built a strong reputation in building new organizations and revitalizing low-performing organizations while providing a superior customer experience. Erin has received numerous awards in recognition of her success. She has found her passion that drives her: helping others build personal and professional cultures. Erin possesses a Bachelor of Science in business management and an MBA.

Raised in Connecticut and now residing in southern New Jersey, Erin enjoys sports, travel, entertaining, spending time with friends and family, and planning events. She is working to get herself back to that confident, sassy, and fearless three-year-old, ready to take on the world. Erin shares important lessons learned along the way that are crucial for all of us to know so we don't lose that strong confidence we are all born with. Though there is more work to do, Erin is determined to give others hope and inspire them to live the life they desire. She is building her legacy as she continues her journey to capture that confidence back. Follow her journey through her social media channels to learn more from her and how you can connect and work with her.

To connect with Erin

www.themccahillgroup.com
em@themccahillgroup.com
Facebook: www.facebook.com/erinamccahillmba
Instagram: @erinamccahillmba
LinkedIn: www.linkedin.com/in/erinamccahillmba

REBIRTH

Debbie Pettit

"You can't go back and change the beginning, but you can start where you are and change the ending."

—C. S. Lewis

On a snowy, blustery November day, a sweet, innocent baby girl was born into this world to two people who had pasts of trauma and abuse and generational wounds held deep within their souls. They were living a life of covering up lies to just appease their families. This beautiful baby born to them was a pawn, meant to cover up the true life they were living—a life of deceit—in hopes things would change for the better once she was born. Debbie, younger self.

Having anxiety and PTSD is something I would never wish on anyone. I can't do this. I can't take the constant bombardment of negative, scary thoughts that send my mind spiraling deep into hell and my body into an anxious, fearful mess. Every day, every moment, I work hard to thwart the evil thoughts put into my head, and yet no one would ever know as I push through each day and night as if nothing were wrong. I have not been completely healed of my lifetime of trauma. I have been retriggered. Debbie, present day.

Does a two-year-old know that it is wrong to poop on the floor? Does a two-year-old being potty trained need to be beat for pooping on the floor? This is the very first memory I have of my father. And so it begins . . .

As an only child, I was thrust into the care of my dying mother who had cancer. I was watching her die a slow death. My stepfather had cancer at the same time as well. I desperately did what I could for my mother and stepfather as they battled this horrific illness. This was the same mother I tried to protect from my abusive father for years. You see, since I was a child, I tried to keep my mother safe from harm. And now I could not. I had no control over the inevitable. The trauma of it all sucked me into the darkness of my mind. PTSD.

Leave me, leave me to be raised by others I barely know. Maybe this was a good thing? All I know is that I was dropped off at babysitters from the age of four until I was twelve years old as my parents worked. Not my choice, especially when I barely knew the people watching me. It was uncomfortable as a child. But, considering the fact that my father was abusive to me both physically and mentally and my mother never protected me from this violent man, maybe it was best I be with babysitters.

Having your mother pass and being so traumatized over it all and not being able to bring yourself to attend her viewing and barely making it through the funeral. Anxiety had taken over, and I hit a wall. Guilt had set in. I was not with her when she died. I was too scared to witness her last hours.

Two little eyes and one frightened child witnessing two parents argue and fight constantly. Objects being thrown at my mom, clothes being ripped off, my dad hitting my mom, my mom's bruised face, phones being pulled off the wall, my phone calls to the police. *Scared* is not the right word to describe my terrorized mind. Running in my room to stay away from my father, praying that the hitting and yelling would stop. Afraid for my mom and my life.

Our second child was born, a little girl only weighing four pounds, thirteen ounces. Born on March 13 at 7:13 p.m. with a condition called Ring Chromosome 13, she could not walk or talk and would have a lifetime of challenges. This was a child who would teach everyone about unconditional love. This child stole the hearts of everyone around her with her beautiful smile and hugs. We were so devoted to taking care of this precious child who passed when she was a few weeks shy of her twenty-third birthday. We were told she would not live past the age of one. April.

I was not allowed to be seen or heard. "Stop crying or I will give you a reason to cry." A father's pure frustration over being locked into generational wounds and him taking it out on his child led to a foot shoved up my rear end and being hit for no reason at all. I was a child deathly afraid of her father, fearing his existence in her world. Lying in bed awake at night, scared for him to come home for fear he would start a fight with my mom. Then I would have to lie there feeling helpless and scared.

The phone call from your mother-in-law shortly after your handicapped child was born telling you that the reason your child is handicapped is because you exercised and didn't eat right when you were pregnant with her. Needless to say, I had years of battles with that narcissist, self-centered, controlling mother-in-law. Didn't work well with my marriage as her children and husband were victims and oblivious to her manipulative, evil ways; they were all controlled by her. It was their way of life. They didn't know anything different.

Going to school, being teased, laughed at, and bullied by my classmates because I was fat, as they told me. Being beat up walking home from school because I was fat. Being picked last for teams out on recess because I was fat. Never going to prom.

Being twenty years old and told that your father was gay and your mother knew it when she married him in hopes that he would change. Feeling like a pawn, used as a front to cover up the lie he lived. This explained part of why my father was violent and angry. The other part I was eventually told is that my paternal grandparents beat him as a child and locked him in a dark attic by himself for punishment. Generational wounds.

Generational wounds, anxiety, PTSD. You think?! Living a childhood without love but with physical and verbal abuse that caused constant stress that led into an adulthood full of traumas that never had a good ending has led me to trying to figure out how I could finally live a *free* life, a life full of joy and abundance! I was longing to live a life where there was no anxiety holding me back from living my best life, a life where I was not skeptical about living, but I was stuck between listening to my own horrible thoughts, which were, "I am a prisoner of my anxiety forever, for the rest of my life," and knowing that I am free and I have always been free. But still, I was unable to move forward without being stuck in fear and anxiety. How was I going to shift my mindset from gloom and doom to bright and sunny? I only wish I could start my life all over again. I wanted a second chance! I knew there was a missing link.

My anxiety had gotten so bad I could barely sleep at night. I prayed and prayed. "Please, dear God, just let me sleep, just give me a few hours so my mind can think clearly and I can go through my day with clarity, calmness, and energy." I finally drifted off to sleep.

A beautiful meadow with flowers blowing in the wind, flowers of many vivid colors, calming and peaceful. A mountain in the background that seemed to have a golden hue to it, an aura around this mountain that kept calling me to walk closer and closer. As I moved forward, I felt there was a power, energy that I had to follow. It was coming from the top of the mountain. As I looked upward and kept climbing, I could see this shiny, glittery object that looked like a castle! It kept calling me to come closer and closer. As I neared the top, I could see it was a castle with doors opening up for me the closer I got. These doors had a golden, calming glow that was pulling me into them. An energy I could not resist, a peaceful energy filled with love. I stopped, I wanted to take all of this in. Looking up through these doors, I could see something moving toward me. As it got closer, I could see a figure of a girl, more like an angelic figure. It was. It was a beautiful, sparkly, glowing angel! It was my daughter, April! How could this be? I was speechless. She then reached out to me; she had something she was giving me. It was a golden heart. *Baby girl, what are you trying to tell me?*

"This is your opportunity to claim love for yourself and to protect yourself from everything else. This is your opportunity to make a stand and say, 'No more!' You need to fully love and accept yourself. You are okay, you are going to get through this. Everything you need right now is inside of you. It's time to come back home to yourself and the love inside you." April helped me understand love like I never had in my life—unconditional. She was here to fill the hole of unconditional love, love as a child I did not know. It never was part of my life until April. She was sending the message to me that now I get to choose to show up for myself and love myself regardless that no one else ever had. I get to show up right now in this moment!

I needed to get back. I needed to talk to my younger self to tell her everything was going to be okay. When I found my younger self in my dream, I told her this.

"Come, come sit with me, little one. Here are some things that you need to know to help you along the way. No one was ever there to tell you, 'I love you.' No one was ever there for you to tell you, 'You are worthy and I am here to tell you that you are!' We can't go back and change the beginning, but we can start where we are and change the ending. We must heal, we must release the grief over a childhood, a relationship that we never had with parents. All these traumas are just packed inside of us.

We need to cry. We need to grieve to create space for healing and love. We need to stand in our own voice. We are now protected, grounded, and safe! It is now time, time to step into our confidence. It's time for us to step into our power. It is time for us to truly and completely love ourself, and it is time for us to come home to ourself."

My younger self then looked at me and said, "But look at you! Look what you've been through! Look at your perseverance and how strong you are! Look at your strength, persistence, perseverance, presence, and the way you show up for others! Thank you for all you have done. I love you too!"

The sun was shining, the rays of warmth were beaming onto my face, and the birds were singing. I opened my eyes from such a deep, wonderful sleep and felt a peace like I had never before.

One day you wake up and you're in this place.
You're in this place where everything feels right.
Your heart is calm. Your soul is lit.
Your thoughts are positive.
Your vision is clear.
You're at peace, at peace with where you've been,
at peace with what you've been through,
and at peace with where you're headed.

ABOUT DEBBIE PETTIT

Debbie Pettit is a #1 international best-selling author, personal trainer, lifestyle transformational coach, weight loss coach, and group fitness instructor. During her extensive fitness career, she was the owner of Lady Fitness Health Spa, an award-winning women's fitness and wellness center. She also has online businesses called Fit Girls For Life and Success Within where she mentors and coaches clients through their weight loss journey and does online workouts.

Debbie has been very active in local organizations and volunteering in her community and was the first female to run as mayor in her town where she was narrowly defeated. She founded "April's Run," a 5K event designed to raise funds for families with financial hardships who have children with long-term illnesses and hospital stays at The Children's Hospital of Philadelphia. In honor and memory of her daughter, April, who passed away in 2007 in the Children's Hospital, Debbie formed the April Nicole Pettit Memorial Fund.

Debbie has also been the recipient of The Salem County Women of Achievement Award in recognition of her positive impact upon the quality of life of the citizens of Salem County through her remarkable record of community leadership and volunteerism, as well as her significant contributions to the community, which also commended her as a woman of remarkable character and exceptional determination.

Debbie's passion, besides mentoring those in their wellness journey, is to help and support others who are suffering from trauma, anxiety, depression, and PTSD by encouraging positivity, empowerment, and self-love to achieve their personal best and live their life to the fullest.

To connect with Debbie

dpettitcoaching@gmail.com
Facebook: Fit Girls For Life or Debbie Pettit, Woodstown, NJ
Instagram: @ladyfitness00

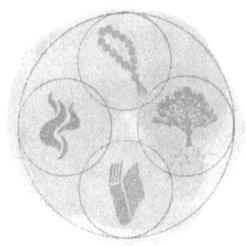

LIFE BEFORE RUTHLESS

Samantha Ruth

A month or so ago, my brother called me with my parents and my nieces in the background. I could hear the restrained laughter in his voice as he asked (already knowing my answer), "Who do you think Dad's favorite is?"

Him! Obviously!

(My mom's, too, for the record.)

It turns out, my dad was somehow under the impression that I think it's me.

In what universe?

Let me tell you about my universe.

I live in a universe where my dad has never told me that he's proud of me. As in, literally, not once. In over forty-nine years. My mom tells me all the time to try to make up for my dad.

We're close now, me and my mom. The key word being *now*. Growing up, it was a very different story.

I hear my friends' stories of crying as they drop their kids off for their first day of school. In my universe, my mom went home and threw a party. Okay, maybe not a real party, but she absolutely celebrated.

When I left for college, I promise you, it was a real party.

And my dad? My dad always wanted a boy. As much as I tried to be a little version of him, I would never be a boy. So I was definitely Daddy's little girl, but purely by default.

So I'm the girl who never felt good enough. Anywhere. The girl who never really belonged. Anywhere.

Everywhere.

I'm the girl others expected to move mountains. The girl who expects even more from herself.

I'm the girl who grew up not being allowed to make mistakes. The girl who accepted nothing less than perfection. The girl who grew up way too fast—because she had no other choice.

I'm the girl who was taught that love has conditions. That to be loved means to do things their way. That doing things your own way means people withdraw their love and affection.

Until Jim.

And our story is a story of its own.

Suffice it to say, I received the kind of fairytale love I thought only existed in the movies. The kind without conditions. Without strings. And it taught me how I deserve to be treated. How we all deserve to be treated.

Support and encouragement don't always come from the people we want it from the most. But that doesn't mean it's not there from others. It doesn't mean we can't find it within ourselves!

It took losing Jim for me to reevaluate everything. Myself. My future. My friends. My everything. It took being in such deep pain for me to not only find the answers but to actually stop and ask myself the questions.

Why am I doing this? Am I doing this for me or because others want me to? Do I even know what I want?

I became absolutely Ruthless about healing. About living life my way. About being my true self, not who anyone else expects me to be.

About doing things I enjoy. Being with people I enjoy.

About *not* doing things or being with people I don't enjoy.

Up until that point, we'll call it Life Before Ruthless, life wasn't about any of these things. Not even a little.

For the first time in my life, I was taking care of me—without worrying about what my family or friends or colleagues thought and expected.

And guess what?

I wish I did it sooner. I realized that Life Before Ruthless wasn't really living. I figured out things that no one ever taught me. The lessons that are more important than anything we can ever learn in books and classrooms.

First and foremost: You. Are. Enough.

Period.

You are enough. Exactly as you are.

I can't say it too many times. You can't hear it too many times. The world doesn't always tell us that we're enough the way we are. The people we need to hear it from the most might never tell you.

So I'll say it again because it's easy to get distracted and confused by all the outside noise.

You. Are. Enough.

Write it down. Say it out loud. Remember it when life gets noisy.

Because there is noise, literally everywhere. All the time. And it can be quiet, barely noticeable noise. Or it can be blaring noise loud enough for the world to hear. Either way, it drowns out the only voice that matters—your own—if you're not paying attention.

So tune out the noise! And remember that it's everywhere!

There's noise from our parents. From our families. Expectations. Traditions. The specific noise is different for each of us. But it's there for all of us. That college legacy, the family business, the way you behave in public.

There's noise at school. From the teachers, from your friends. What to wear. What not to wear. What's in and what's out. Even where to sit for lunch.

There's noise from the media. Whether it's your favorite shows, songs, or celebrities, the messages are there. The commercials. The advertisements. All of it.

There's noise from the world—whether we like it or listen to it or not. Boys don't cry and girls don't play football. Stereotypes. Expectations.

Noise.

Tune it out!

It's so important for you to stay in touch with what you're doing. With why you're doing it. Is it really for you, or has the noise influenced your choices?

Make time to check in with yourself. To slow down. To feel. Your body knows if you're off course. Listen to it. Pay attention to the clues. Beware of the noise.

Along the way, you need to know that mistakes *will* happen. It's an absolute part of life. It's how we grow. Know that mistakes do *not* define you. It's about how you respond after the mistakes.

So don't beat yourself up for your mistakes like I did. And don't let other people use your mistakes against you. Ever!

You're human; therefore, you'll make mistakes. It's that simple. And guess what?

Mistakes are fun!

I'm not kidding. I absolutely missed out on the fun of life because I was so wrapped up in getting things done the right way. I didn't enjoy the experiences. The moments. The lessons. The laughter.

Let yourself have fun. Don't take things so seriously. Don't take life so seriously. And definitely don't take yourself so seriously!

You'll miss out on so many adventures!

And perfection is unattainable. That's something I never heard and I really want you to hear. There is absolutely no such thing as perfect.

So striving for perfection is an insane cycle of disappointments.

Let it go. Accept that living includes failing. Allow yourself to mess up and learn and, most importantly, have fun.

I need to take another moment to remind you again about the noise. Because it's always there. There will be people saying you're too much of this and not enough of that.

People judging. People offering opinions. Remember that this is your life, no one else's. It's so important for you to be you, your true self, not who anyone else wants or expects you to be.

You'll find your people. The ones who lift you up. The ones who really see you. The ones who cheer you on. The ones who accept and embrace you for you.

Like Jim.

Surround yourself with these people.

Because there are also people who will mock you. People who will try to silence you. People who think your dreams are too big.

Remember that this is just more noise. And these are their issues and a reflection of their character, not a reflection of you and your character.

You need to know that love isn't conditional. It's not a transaction, and it doesn't have strings.

Real love means not only accepting someone for who they are. It also means being accepted for who you are!

It means being yourself—completely. With flaws and imperfections. And being loved because of those imperfections, not in spite of them!

You read that correctly. It means being loved because of those imperfections, not in spite of them.

So embrace your quirks. Know that what makes you different makes you beautiful. The things you see as flaws and weaknesses are, in reality, your superpowers.

For me, it's my anxiety. The world says my anxiety is something "wrong" with me. I spent years judging myself, trying to "fix" it. And then, after losing Jim, I was in so much pain that I honestly didn't care.

I embraced it and realized that the world is wrong. Plain and simple.

My anxiety makes me me. It makes me aware of my surroundings. It allows me to empathize with others in a way that most not only don't, but most don't even understand.

Whether it's an illness or a birthmark or anything in between, your quirks make you you. And that is your biggest strength.

Being you.

No matter what the noise says.

Because boys do cry and girls can play football. Your dreams are never too big. And your mistakes are part of life, not weapons to be used against you. Live life your way knowing that real love is unconditional. Period.

And hold the people like Jim close. Be the person who lifts others up and cheers them on and accepts them exactly as they are. Treasure these relationships.

Because losing Jim also meant that I lost that person. That support. That feeling of someone always having my back.

I now have others in my life who are like Jim. But no one will ever be Jim. He's the person who's the most proud of me. The person who believes in me when I don't believe in myself. The person who really and truly sees me.

He's my strength. My confidence. My everything. Even with him physically gone, he's still the reason behind everything I do. My why. And making *him* proud, not my dad, is my motivation.

When I originally committed to this book, I planned to have a serious conversation with my dad. I was going to ask him if he's proud of me. (I guarantee he'd dispute the fact that he's never told me in the first place.)

I spent my Life Before Ruthless trying to gain his approval. Gain his affection. Eagerly hoping to hear those four special words.

Since Becoming Ruthless,[1] I've let all of that go. And it's empowering! But I still was considering at least expressing myself and having the conversation.

But something happened through writing this . . . I've realized that the conversation isn't what's important. His view of me isn't what's important.

What's important is my view of myself. What's important is that I'm so unbelievably proud of myself. And that's not something I've allowed myself to feel very often.

Which is another reminder: celebrate your wins. All of them. Big and small. Be proud of your accomplishments. Be proud of who you are.

I know who I am. I know what I've been through. I know what I stand for. And I also know that I'm absolutely enough. Exactly as I am.

It took redefining myself. It took Redefining Ruthless for me to learn these life lessons, and I don't want anyone else to go a day without knowing them because they're the most valuable lessons I've learned in life. ♡

Stay tuned for *Redefining Ruthless*, available this spring/summer 2023.

Redefining Ruthless: This is my process of owning who I am without worrying about who others want me to be. It's about embracing my quirks rather than trying to change them. It's the process I used to eliminate any and all toxins from my life, including people! It's my way of being completely true to myself . . . ruthlessly!

So this negatively charged word now has a positive space, and this is how I live my life. Helping people transform their perceived negatives into their biggest strengths.

Redefining Ruthless, available this spring/summer 2023.

1—"Becoming Ruthless" is my chapter in *Faces Of Mental Illness*, available here: www.facesofmentalillness.com.

ABOUT SAMANTHA RUTH

Samantha is a psychologist, speaker, best-selling author, and host of *The Be Ruthless Show*, a podcast dedicated to making noise and breaking stigmas. She helps people around the world turn their pain into their power by guiding them to be their true selves, not who they think they need to be, by embracing their differences and recognizing that their perceived weaknesses are their biggest strengths, and by living life on their own terms.

Samantha's mission is to change the way the world views both grief and mental health so people can speak about whatever issues they have and get the help they not only need but deserve without fear of judgment, labels, or repercussions.

Samantha is the proud founder of Griefhab, a 24/7 community open to anyone who has experienced a loss. After losing her husband, Sam learned personally how little support is available and vowed to create these services for others.

In her free time, you can find Sam and her pups, Sassy and Dallas, on one of their outdoor adventures. They love living in Colorado and never miss an opportunity to explore their beautiful surroundings. Music fuels Sam's soul, family means everything to her, and honoring her late husband, Jim, and making him proud gives her life daily purpose.

To connect with Sam

samantharuth.com
sam@samantharuth.com

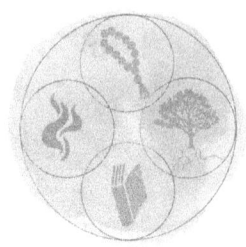

POETRY FOR MY SOUL

Ericha Scott, PhD, LPCC917, LAADC, ATR-BC, REAT

"Freud . . . credited the poets with discovering the unconscious before he did, and referred to poets as 'those few to whom it's given to salvage from the whirlpool of their emotions the deepest truths to which we others have to force our way, ceaselessly groping among torturing uncertainties.'"

—Morris R. Morrison, *Poetry as Therapy*

What I can tell you, without any caveats, is how much poetry and the arts have helped me throughout my life-span while at the same time providing joy, insight, purpose, and meaning.

As a licensed psychotherapist and a dually certified creative and expressive arts therapist with thirty-eight years of experience, I have seen a variety of the arts help heal clients with complex trauma, substance and behavioral use disorders, and mental illness. The creative arts, facilitated in my office, have helped reach and heal clients who have repeatedly failed treatment with previous providers. Often, these vulnerable people were considered to be hopeless when referred to my practice.

Although it is not commonly known, in some ways, I was

considered to be hopeless. I was born with significant fetal alcohol effects at a time when secrets were more important than interventions. I was born with a cleft palate, hearing loss, minor cranial facial deformities, a compromised immune system, severe allergies, and a failure to thrive.

My mother explained that she had to pinch me when I was an infant to make me open my mouth so that I could eat. She also explained that she would squirt baby formula into my mouth after she pinched me because I could not suckle.

I remained significantly underweight until college.

As you can imagine, my school experience was a disaster. You might *not* be able to imagine that school remained a disaster—until I began taking art classes and writing poetry.

While in hospice, my mother said, "We never thought you would have a normal life. I am so glad to see what you have accomplished." This was an enormous admission for her to make.

When I met my husband, Randy Tufts, in my midforties, he could not see evidence of what I have just told you. I said, "Okay, I understand, so when mother visits, I will ask her in front of you if she thought I was 'retarded' as a child."

So, I did this.

Randy was driving, and my mother was sitting in the front passenger seat. I was sitting in the back, in the middle, so I could see them both. Casually, I said, "So, Mom, when I was little, you thought I was retarded, right?" She responded with, "Oh yes, you were stupid." I said, "So you understand that this is no longer true since I have a doctorate and UCLA has published my research?" Without missing a beat, she said, "No, honey, there is still something."

I failed fourth grade and nearly failed it twice until my mother hired a private art teacher for me. After a year or more of art lessons and a few months of reading adult science fiction out loud to my stepmother, my reading comprehension improved—and progressed all the way—to college level.

Carl Jung referred to creative experiential therapies, "imaginative action" (writing, movement, and visual art), as having a powerful healing impact. I concur.

One valuable aspect of the creative arts therapies is "cathartic release." When a therapy or workshop participant finds the correct symbol or work(s) to describe their inner world, they experience relief.

I barely remember the lines of my first poem. I know the themes had to do with nature and God. I tentatively handed my poem to my English teacher after class was dismissed. She was busy with too many students, and it seemed as if she hardly noticed until she approached me with kindness and praise. I was around twelve years old, which means I now have been writing poetry for fifty-six years. The themes of my poems are very much the same today: nature, God, and love. It might be more accurate to say nature, God, love—and transcendence after trauma.

It is difficult to comprehend the reason for this, but people who have experienced a difficult birth are more likely to embrace metaphysical concepts. I fit this category. Fortunately, I am also able to take an objective view and consider the possibility that I am wrong. That said, my life would be much less rich, rewarding, and interesting without my belief in miracles. Quite frankly, even if we find hard scientific proof about why I was able to progress from being "retarded" (my mother's word, not mine) to bright and some say brilliant, I am still a miracle.

The creative arts allow us to own the whole spectrum and continuum of our compartmentalized polarities of life and self. Poetry, photography, painting, the processes, and the art product show us a mysterious educational PowerPoint of the psyche in a way that helps us make sense of what seems invisible. One of the many blessings of inner-depth work via the creative and expressive arts is a return to the integrated self, the person we were always meant to be.

I am fortunate; I have experienced two great loves in my life.

My husband, Randy Tufts, was a soulmate, a wonderful husband, and an outstanding human being. He died tragically due to illness in 2003. I had been a therapist for years before we met, and when he died, I took time to take care of myself, attend grief workshops, and honor his memory in a multitude of ways over several decades. In addition, I made art, including a mask of my grieving self, and I wrote poems about him. For years, I have missed my beautiful husband and simultaneously arrived at a place of peace. I was fortunate to walk by his side every step of the way.

In 1978, 1979, and 1982, when I was twenty-five to twenty-eight years old, I spent significant time in two small ancient French villages while a student and later as an assistant to Monsieur Jean-Pierre Cannelle. Jean-Pierre was the photography teacher for the Lacoste School of the Arts.

Now, I am sixty-eight years old, a crone, and integration is the gift I received last year during the pandemic as I delved into the loss of another great love. This was not my plan. I thought of my time in southern France at age twenty-eight as far away in the past, as if it was a previous lifetime. I felt removed from it. I knew it had been a significant and magical time; sadly, like with my husband Randy, it also had a tragic ending. The tragedy was not my fault, nor the fault of my fiancé, a French farmer named Michel.

In 2021, while isolated during the pandemic, Michel—the spirit of Michel—seemed to appear to me. I doubt this visitation would have been able to occur if I had been living my normal, busy pre-pandemic lifestyle. I have seen ghosts since I was a child, so I was not frightened but instead curious. I decided to explore what this was about, even contemplating that my experience might be simply a projection of myself. Even so, I allowed myself to feel his presence, love, and yearning, and I began to weep. I don't cry much or often, so it was a surprise to me that I cried for eight months. Those tears were the best letter I could have written to my younger self.

This chapter, my poems, and my photography document how I have chosen to bear witness to myself as a young twenty-eight-year-old woman and, by doing so, honor her with reverence, love, and respect. This is the foundation of integration. The best definition of integration, as I mean it here, is making one whole out of the conscious and unconscious.

Adam Blatter, MD, states, "The process of personal growth and development involves many aspects of the human experience where the expressive arts serve as channels for integrating—intellect and imagination, sensation and emotion, mind and body."[1]

As I left France in 1982, I remember standing next to Michel as we locked the door of his house that last morning. I was engaged, deeply, passionately in love, and happier than I had ever been. At the time, I planned to return to France to marry a few months later. I had no idea that morning that I would never see Michel again in this lifetime.

At age twenty-eight, I had no time to grieve due to a series of tragedies clustered all in a row. I was too busy surviving.

MULTIDIMENSIONAL PHOTOGRAPH—October 2021

Stained with fixative,
lost or packed away
I still search for that photo,
for memories of your touch
and your breath
in the silver emulsion
that shiny, cold, flat dimensional space
to remember how you matched my heartbeat
the moon's energetic pull
and ocean tides
how your skin smelled like the earth
after the rain
and how you blushed when you proposed
on one knee, in front of your friends
in that dark, dank café
such a public gesture for such a private man
in the café, my Taj Mahal, where our love was enshrined
and I have no photographs of you.
It was not your fault, my love, nor mine.
That dinged wooden chair where I sat, felt like a throne.
What I wanted to photograph, cannot be seen
by the eyes or a lens.
Your love for me remains more tangible
than a photograph
held in my hand
under the gaze
of my loop.
I am an old woman now,
and I have not forgotten the hidden canister
of undeveloped film

full of latent images
from our un-lived life
together, nor
our heartbeats,
your touch, and
the smell of your skin.

As the energetic visitations continued, I began to search for Michel in real life via the internet, old friends, and hand-written letters to the mayors of several small towns in France. Honestly, after a while, I became tired of looking at online pictures of balding old French men with reddish frizzy hair, green eyes, and cleft chins. One night in frustration, I decided to stop everything, the grieving, the looking, the art. I was *done*. I could not think of one good reason to continue this quest.

The next morning, I woke up with a very vivid, powerful dream message. My subconscious, my twenty-eight-year-old self, was *not* done! So, I continued. Fortunately, my fatigue left; I felt reinvigorated by the dream.

CROSSROADS—October 9, 2021

Dressed in colors of Alchemy
you arrive in my sleeping dreams
as a holy black man.
I am sitting at the white table waiting.
You offer me a bowl of courage
in front of an empty street,
as you tenderly whisper
the word in my ear, with a French accent.
Janus and Hecate would laugh out loud together
while holding hands.
I never could learn the meaning of the word "carrefour"
no matter how many times you said it.
Freud would say it was a "block."

Nevertheless, I took a sip,
I swallow the elixir because
I am in love with a ghost
or a shadow of memory.
Decades after I lost you,
my new husband died.
I have never been lucky in love.
Once a woman compared the pain of her divorce to my
    husband's death.
She said, "At least you know he loved you."
I thought, *This woman has never loved.*
I am a "sacred fool," I speak uncomfortable truths,
you taught me this,
and it seems as if you watch me and whisper
through a one-way mirror
as I live and search for you
in between two worlds.

IMPRINT—October 11, 2021

"Tu fais l'amour avec ton âme."
I never knew anyone else who could do that
or would.
You asked me to look in your eyes,
not "at" or "into,"
I was more compliant then.
Slowly you called out my soul from her hiding places
the haystack, the barn, the attic, the basement,
maybe even a coffin.
She blinked, adjusting to the light,
and felt your love.
Starving and nearly blind from a life sentence of isolation,
    you fed her
what the heart, soul, and body needs.
You knew she was innocent and wrongfully punished.

When I left France, I put her back into hiding
She went willingly; she was so bereft.
This time I gave her a candle,
in hindsight, such an inadequate gift.
It was not an appropriate light for a haystack or the world.
I burned myself up.
I was plunged into a darkness that still takes my breath away.
It nearly took my life,
the myth that I was safer in my own country
than a young woman on foreign soil.
You tried to warn me gently not to go home for a few months,
that request did not make sense to me,
how did you know what I could not see?
This year, my soul heard your voice and felt your presence
    decades later.
She emerged once again, like Persephone, looking for you
    in springtime,
and disappointed, she only found me.
I have so much compassion for her, my lost soul.
We both want to thank you and ask for your forgiveness.

THE STONE WELL—January 4, 2022

I am a woman standing at the well of time.
I dip my ladle into the source
to find reflections
on the liquid surface.
I gaze inside the silver cup
to see hints of another life.
The memories come,
unbidden and unchained.
"Haven't I got enough of my own?"
The Samaritan woman
seemed to know what she was doing.
She drank from the living waters.
I don't, or do I?
My divining rod turned the wrong direction.
It went up.
The Provencal men laughed,
and slapped their knees with their berets.
I was busy walking across the Ley Lines
and missed the joke,
and the tiny black poodle
kept digging for truffles
by the gnarled roots.
The men from Roussillon said,
"It will always go up for you
for the rest of your life,
it will always go up."
The city stones blush rouge for me.
It is nighttime in southern France.
There is a bright light
illuminating the darkest shadows.
I find this odd and out of place.
Where is the source of light?
I look behind me and see nothing.

I look at my feet, and
there is no shadow
for my silhouette.
I am standing in the valley
where I first fell in love with you.
The vineyards are hidden just out of view.
I smell the lush dirt and the old, wet leaves.
It is autumn.
Once I asked you, "What is your favorite season?"
You tilted your head and shrugged,
"I have to say, 'Winter, spring, summer, and fall.'"
You are not you, but I know who you are.
You are a farmer and a mason, fit but stocky,
with large hands.
This is ironic since your features were so refined.
I have not figured out this part of the dream yet.
The circular wall is short but wide.
And the field stones
seem as old as Jerusalem.
There is a metal cover
sealing the fountain.
I cannot see the markings.
They look unfamiliar and ancient.
You lift the cover off by yourself,
a Herculean feat,
to reveal access
to the current
that flows underground.
To find the depth,
the meaning,
you drop large rocks
into the center.
We wait,
but there is no sound.

There is no bottom.
The well is fathomless.
The fluid glistens black
and sparkles like stars.
What does it mean
that the well is filled with fossil oil?
I do not know what to make of this,
and while I am thinking,
you suddenly jump in over your head.
I lean back in surprise.
Then, one black, oil-covered hand
reaches up and out to grab more rocks.
You stretch your arm and grope blindly,
to find bigger, heavier rocks
from the ledge and the ground.
Still no bottom.
I think of the Black Madonna.
the Magdalene of Languedoc,
and although you must doubt it,
I loved you the way she loved Jesus.
I would have washed your dry and cracked
feet with precious and expensive oils.
Is this how we find the mysteries?
Is this how I fix my mistakes?
The Ley Lines
from forty years ago
drag my heart
across the ocean floor
and again from underneath
Chartres to Bonnieux, while
the three Marys weep for me.
I tumble and roll in the currents,
holding my breath,
from the past to the future,

and back again.
Alas, Barrett was Judas,
my father was Pilate,
my grandfather Herod,
and a friend
was the greatest betrayer of all.
But then there you are
suddenly standing by the well again
perfectly clean, as if purified,
transformed by immersion,
sanctified by the anointing oil,
and my tears.
I was astonished and delighted,
I want to shout that there has been
miraculous healing!
This has been an answer to my prayers
for your well-being.
Then, in the typical way that
I mix the sacred and the temporal,
I find that I feel so relieved
that I will not have to do
your laundry tonight.
I shake my head
and laugh at myself.
Yet, like the apostles, I want to tell the world
you are alive; I have seen you,
you have been resurrected
and you are going to be all right.
You were my anointed. You carried the lineage of
the holy for me.
And still, I have no idea why this happened in 2021.
Why you, when you are so far away from me,
and why now . . .
and why not then
when I needed you so?

In 2022, I returned to our small village in Provence, France, for the first time in forty years. The greatest irony, or synchronicity, is that the people who knew and remembered Michel best were the landlords of the small studio I had rented online. Although strangers to me, they were kind and empathetic to my search. They described Michel as profoundly sensitive. A farmer I had known years before, George, asked the previous mayor about Michel to find out that he had died years ago. This was not a surprise. My doctoral internship with Dr. Gary E. Schwartz at the University of Arizona included studies regarding the validity of mediumship.

The visitations from Michel, especially over such a prolonged duration, fit better into the framework of mediumship and channeling than other possibilities. Although, I do not close my mind to other realities.

Below is a photo of the objects I took to France, a block of myrrh that I bought in Israel years ago, a large rose quartz, and snake vertebrae to bury in the earth to honor Michel's life and what he meant to me. Snake vertebrae have been found in ancient burial sites around the world, and in Texas where I was born, along with carvings of snakes on bone. Because snakes shed their skins, they often represent transition, life, death, rebirth, and eternal life—and, in some traditions, passion. Myrrh was used in the Hebrew bible as an anointing and embalming oil, as you read hints about in my last poem. The meaning of the heart-shaped rose quartz is self-explanatory.

What I find interesting is how many of my very close friends have felt and noticed a positive shift or change in me since I returned from my journey. I feel more whole. I have reclaimed some of the hope, wonderment, and wanderlust of my youth without having to work at it. I have more vigor. I am more at peace with my life station and more content with my age and aging. This could seem contradictory, but it makes perfect sense to me. The logic of the subconscious is very different from that of the conscious mind. This is all to say thank you to my twenty-eight-year-old self for not giving up on me and for her willingness to participate in this journey together. I did not know how much I had missed her. I did not understand until now that when I lost Michel, I had also lost her.

This is a journey that is best served with a mentor guide. If you would like support in creative, expressive, meaningful, and spiritual transformational processes such as what I have described here, please call me at 310-880-9761. I offer private creative arts intensives in my office here in Malibu, or group intensives with like-minded people anywhere in the world.

1—Morris R. Morrison (ed.), *Poetry as Therapy* (New York, NY: Human Sciences Press, Inc., 1987).

ABOUT ERICHA SCOTT, PHD, LPCC917, LAADC, ATR-BC, REAT

Dr. Scott has been a healer who has walked the fine line between mysticism and evidenced-based psychotherapy for thirty-eight years. She is a licensed clinical professional counselor (LPCC917) and is certified as a substance use disorder counselor, interfaith spiritual director, Reiki master, and a dually certified creative and expressive arts therapist. She is a published poet, artist, international best-selling author, and keynote speaker.

Dr. Scott is a fellow for the oldest trauma organization in the world, The International Society for the Study of Trauma and Dissociation, and is an expert in grief, trauma, dissociation, self-harm, nightmares, integrative health, and the creative arts psychotherapies.

She designed and facilitated art psychoeducational and creative arts therapeutic workshops for many decades. She has been recognized throughout the United States and abroad for her original, unique, and powerful healing experiences.

Dr. Scott's academic writing and research have been published in trade magazines, textbooks, and peer review journals by *The Journal of Chemical Dependency*, UCLA, Oxford University Press, and Taylor and Francis.

To learn more, please visit her website at www.artspeaksoutloud. org. To book her for individual creative arts intensive in her office in Malibu, as a keynote speaker, or as a group retreat leader, please get in touch with her directly at 310-880-9761.

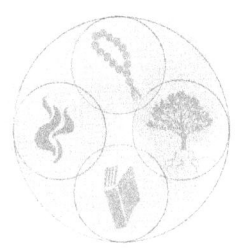

WALK THE TALK.
PREVENTION IS BETTER THAN CURE!

Raida Abdulsalam Abu-Issa

*"Life is like a piano: What you get out of it
depends on how you play it."*

—Tom Lehrer

Dear younger me, Rourou,

Let's talk! Not that boring blame game kind of talk when others usually want to complain about something. Let's have a real talk, between Rourou & Raida. Talk heart to heart!

I was you and you were me.

My life started at your age like an empty canvas. Moment after moment, phases of excitement, joy, pain, tears, love, fun, shame, hurt, disappointments, and achievements.

Who are you?

Rourou, you are a kaleidoscope by nature that can't live in boxes and with limitations, who loves to explore, travel, and fly to places with new dimensions. You are progressive, yet conservative. Rooted and grounded with your own recipe of values.

Communicating with love and seeing the good in everything is in your DNA.

You are a mix of flavors: Qatari, Palestinian, Lebanese, British, French, and Austrian.

But here we are today wearing different hats: an artist who paints, plays the piano, and loves languages; a certified trainer; a shareholder; and a businesswoman who is an entrepreneur by nature and seeks continuous learning with a growth mindset. We are in the F&B field, and we have ventured in ceramic painting and renewable energy activities. Rich with a plethora of experiences, exposure, beauty, morals, ethics, and cuteness. Come sit next to me and let's watch the movie of our life, an entertaining movie.

Full Circle

Scene 1:

Rourou is dancing joyfully for her father who took her to gatherings among friends where oriental artists performed and played music. She was still a little girl that her father would carry to dance on the table. At times he would carry her and flip her upside down, other times while lying on his bed, he would put her up on his feet. She used to climb on his shoulders to braid his long front hair. He wanted her to get married and live beside him so she could still prepare his special Turkish coffee. She felt so loved and special.

Raida: What's your favorite candy and why?

Rourou: Ice cream in all flavors. To me, it represents youth, coolness, beauty, passion, colorfulness, and playfulness with no restrictions, and helps me connect with my inner self.

Raida: What are your favorite childhood games and what do they mean to you?

Rourou: Elastics game and skipping the rope. They represent flexibility, resilience, movement, desire to play, and curiosity to step outside the norm. Cards, board games, and Monopoly represent strategic thinking, planning, finding solutions by exploring possibilities. Sports like high jumps and running represent overcoming challenges and taking initiatives. Playing with my dolls represent taking care of my younger sibling, finding a way to share my love and care with others.

Raida: What is your favorite character?

Rourou: Tom and Jerry, because they teach playfulness, sneakiness, and friendship and, most importantly, at the end of each episode, they have worked through their conflicts with harmony and love.

Raida: What is your favorite fruit?

Rourou: Apples, because they are at once crunchy, tasty, sweet, and sour. I used to hide some behind the pots in the kitchen cupboard for later.

Scene 2: Glimpses of My Childhood with Family

I have five brothers and one sister, and I'm number six in the family. Whenever I wanted something, I would ask Baba, and he would get it for me. When I was a kid, for some reason I was fixated on this one particular bracelet, and one day I fell ill with high fever, and I insisted on my parents getting it for me. Without thinking, they went out of their way and bought it for me. I felt deeply and unconditionally loved.

Mama installed in me her love for the kitchen while spending time together cooking and baking. I felt lucky because she gave me the freedom to explore recipes at an early age.

My eldest brother would always ask me what I wanted from the bookstore even when he knew that I would ask him the same thing: pencil, eraser, and sharpener. I loved stationery. This made me feel cared for. And later, he became a special person in my husband's life.

My second brother was my go-to person for my math homework. He always reassured me and helped me finish my homework. It meant the world to me then and later in life that I could still go to him for advice in complex situations. He is a problem-solver.

Every time my third brother would come home late from a party, it annoyed him to see me behind the curtain of my room overlooking the entrance of the house. He was terrified that I would tell on him, but I would never do that. He used to drive my sister and I to school. He is supportive.

When I was young, I had partial face paralysis. Later, after I had recovered, I learned that the reason why my fourth brother and my sister used to tell me jokes was to see my funny shifted face. This taught me to take things lightly.

Aida's my older sister and my biggest supporter. I am her biggest fan. I loved spending time with her so much that if she wanted to go to bed earlier than me, I would make her coffee so she could stay up with me as much as possible. She made me feel grounded, and I never doubted that we had each other's back.

Later in life, she was in her third year of university when I was persuaded to go study interior design like her at the same university. I did not enjoy it at the beginning, so I took a few projects from her and just added the letter R before her name so I could submit them as mine under Raida. She made me feel I could trust and rely on her. My mother soon found out.

When my fifth brother was a kid, he decided he did not want a birthday party, but instead, he donated the amount my parents allocated for the party to the poor. This taught me how to be caring and considerate to others.

Scene 3: Your First Life Lessons

Dear Raida,

You are a full-fledged adult now. Your path was beset with challenges that shaped who you are today: Ra'ida, the first to know, astronaut. You have grown to become passionate, loving, caring, genuine, authentic, quite reserved yet warm once trust is established.

When you were ten, you moved from Lebanon to London and learned how to adapt. That was your first big lesson in life.

At the age of eighteen, your father's sudden death was a big shock for you. Your heart was broken immensely, and you felt so alone. You didn't know how to grieve, so you moved on without processing the biggest loss of your life.

Later in university, you wanted to study child psychology and languages but studied interior design like your sister, since it was more convenient. And you learned to accept what life throws at you.

In your late teenage years, you experienced your first love, but also you bottled up your feelings, as it was a taboo to express and share emotions. During that phase, the bond between you two grew stronger as he supported you in your grief after the passing of your father. The connection was strong, strong enough to navigate through the cultural challenges you faced. You did not show emotions toward him or give any commitment before getting your family's approval. To you, relationship and connection are precious, pure, and deep. You needed to make sure there was a light at the end of the tunnel before this relationship even took off. He was your friend, your biggest supporter, and later became the love of your life, your husband, the father of your kids, and your home.

You were twenty-three when you got married. You had five kids and you raised them while running the gifts and fashion jewelry department at your family business. Thirteen years later, you started your own businesses: the first was painting on ceramics (Cafe Ceramique) and the second was a new concept in teaching robotics and renewable energy for youth. Since you were a kid, you had a sense of responsibility; you believed in giving back to the community that was translated later through your aspiration to create a safe space for the youth to unleash their full potential. This taught you to believe in your vision and mission no matter how long the journey is, and that being true to oneself was the only way to live a fulfilling life.

Scene 4:

Dear Raida,

You learned the hard way that if you don't verbalize your emotions and express yourself openly, some people might cross your boundaries and step over you. Your patience and quietness did not serve you either. People did not understand that communication is a skill and an art that should be appreciated, not abused.

You considered it a strength, not a weakness, to choose to be in control of your emotions.

Like everyone else, you had your share of ACEs (adverse childhood experiences) that impacted and channeled your behavior and emotions in certain ways. Some of these experiences were not so significant while others were intense and had long-lasting effects.

When you were in high school, your history teacher once told you that "you will never succeed" because you dropped out of history several times, since English wasn't your first language. Three years later, you graduated with good grades, proving her wrong.

The sudden death of your father was very hard on you during your early adulthood. The impact lasted up till a few years back. It took you many self-development trainings to come to terms with the deep scar that was left behind, and you started identifying where your subconscious fears of loss came from. You wanted your children to enjoy family since nobody knows what tomorrow brings. Your priority in life was first and foremost providing stability, love, and care to your kids, thinking that this would shield them from hardships, losses, and loneliness. You did not want them to go through the pain and void you felt after losing your father. You didn't know that life had a different plan for them. Your intentions to protect the family's well-being at all costs were doubted and interpreted as being controlling.

Scene 5: Losses and Learned Lessons

February 2019—In a strategic move to focus more on less, we decided to sell one of our businesses, but the process of removing my name took longer than expected. A few months later, I came to know that salaries had not been paid for three months and that I was still legally liable. As a result, all our other companies were also blocked, so I had to take extraordinary measures to limit our losses. Then I joined my husband in Austria, and we used our time to think about what was next.

But the surprise came when a few days later, my husband was diagnosed with Stage IV colon cancer. It was shocking and traumatizing news. On top of everything else, it was extremely challenging to find the right treatment plan. After his operation, we were traveling regularly back and forth between Austria and Germany for his treatment. Then, COVID-19 hit and forced us to close our food businesses for a few months, adding to the burden of debt.

Faced with continuous challenges, obstacles, travel bans, and the emotional roller-coaster that comes with it, I was aware of the importance of keeping a positive attitude and a big smile around everyone to protect my children from any additional stress, and keep my husband relaxed during his treatment.

Around the same period, my mother also got sick. Having two sick loved ones with the limitation of travel was the cherry on the top. I lived in continuous fear of losing my mother without seeing her. I couldn't see her for almost a year and a half, but I was lucky enough to have been able to visit her three months before her death.

April 5, 2021—My mother passed away. I was in total shock. I did not have the luxury to fall into pieces. I could not grieve, as I was alone with my husband. I even had to hide from him that she was in intensive care. I felt broken. I wanted to scream. I felt lonely, even my kids couldn't come to support me because of COVID-19 travel restrictions. I had nowhere to go. I did not know what to do. I felt drained. I had nothing left to give.

When my therapist told me that I needed a break, I laughed and asked: "Where and how?"

Eventually, my daughter managed to visit me for emotional support, which allowed me as per the therapist's suggestion, to spend twelve days at a medical spa. At least I had some time to breathe, loosen up, and lash out freely.

Prior to that, I had even accepted to go into therapy with my husband to support his cancer treatment and well-being. Judgmental people surrounded us, questioning our behavior around him and our decision to opt for a holistic treatment. This made it very hard for me to stay focused and strong. The most challenging was to surrender to the doctor's strict instructions, even though it was painful for me to follow.

Adapting to new and tough situations has always been my biggest strength. I have always felt it was my responsibility to adapt, through learning ways to deal with others, being under-standing, giving the benefit of the doubt and excusing people, and being the savior and oxygen for others. I did not anticipate that when one gives too much, they could be taken for granted sometimes and it would become a given for others. At that point, it occurred to me that my cup was empty: I realized that I can't give what I don't have.

Toward the end of 2021, my husband's situation seriously

deteriorated. It was agonizing to see him getting weaker and weaker by the day.

In January 2022, he asked the therapist to come to Doha to support him, but in reality, he planned the support for me. The therapist was guiding me and preparing me to accept the reality of my husband's situation and to let go. It did not make sense to me, and I could not process it. He was hospitalized in January, and I was by his side till his last breath.

February 7, 2022, my husband passed away! I felt numb and was in denial. Even though I have now accepted the harsh reality, I am still going through the ups and downs of grief. I could understand why things happened when they happened and how each training I took and every skill I acquired came in handy at the right time.

Fast-forward to October 2022, life threw another surprise at me. One of the landlords of our businesses with whom we have a close relationship had deposited a guaranteed cheque against rent that bounced and hit my credit. After meeting with the concerned party, I concluded to my son and said: "I'm ready to go through any process even if it goes legal." I was paving the way to live my new chapter in life in freedom with my children.

I chose to not get offended. But for me, enough was enough! Everything came at the same time. I would not stand quiet and patient when it got serious. Limits had been pushed too far. In making conscious decisions to put my inner peace as my top priority, I was choosing to set boundaries. To accept what is, one needs to take a step back to reflect on what's going on and to identify what's next. One needs to channel their emotions, efforts, and put them in the right place.

Scene 6: My Wisdom

My love for learning and expanding my knowledge in child psychology and self-development allowed me to better understand my emotions and triggers and gave me the right tools to explore possibilities to shift and grow. Attending various personal development trainings made me understand the impact of emotions on my well-being and mind. They helped me identify and find my diffuser's mechanism—my painkiller tools rather than giving up and being dependent on anti-depressants. Some of my diffusers are art, journaling, meditation, dancing, yoga, and sports.

I can't be anything but grateful for each and every person who has come into my life, those who are sent to be lessons and those who are true blessings. My experiences were not all bad, because each one had its own flavored lesson that impacted my growth. Therefore, we must make the choice to either stay stuck in the dark or alchemize pain with power. There is gold in pain.

Growth happens over time, not overnight.

The mind is like a magnet. If you think of a blessing, you attract blessings. If you think of problems, you attract problems. Always cultivate good thoughts and try to remain positive. One day, you'll look back and be grateful you did not give up after experiencing all these obstacles in life.

Each one of us is responsible for what we want to create in our life and the world around us. Experiences are happening for us to grow, not to us.

Take one hundred percent responsibility on how you react to events and be the author of your own life.

Notice! We all have some inborn gifts. Explore them and find the right key to your lock to unleash them.

"Don't die with the music still in you!"

—Dr. Wayne Dyer

ABOUT RAIDA ABDULSALAM ABU-ISSA

Raida was born in Qatar, studied in Lebanon until she was ten, and then moved with her family to London. When she was growing up, she learned to adapt and deal with life's sudden changes. After having studied psychology and philosophy in high school, she developed a passion for child psychology and understanding the importance of dealing with emotions and limiting beliefs. Due to the passing of her father at age eighteen, she put her passion on hold as she went on to study interior design and languages in London and Paris. At twenty-one, she returned to Qatar to work at her family business as the Gifts and Fashion Jewelry manager. While excelling in her career, she got married and raised her five children. Entrepreneur by nature, coupled with market knowledge and ambition to bring change, this has allowed Raida to successfully be a part of the quick-changing and challenging market over the years. Her passion for continuous learning and self-development, in addition to her love for child psychology and art, are the fuel that drives Raida's energy. As she moved out of her family business, she launched numerous projects related to entertainment, arts, and food and beverage.

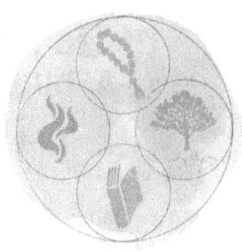

HOME

April Davidson

I look out over the deck and see my oldest daughter, sixteen, swinging in the way back of our country yard. Her head tilted back, her face open to the wind, smiling at the sun. I see her through that faint orange tint of an old 35-mm photograph, which is how memories often surface from my own childhood. She is the picture of youth and of whimsy. At once, I am grateful for her existence and her freedom, as I perceive it, and pained in that profound way that's coupled with nostalgia. I didn't have a swing in my backyard, but acres of lush green grass rolled down a hill, entered the woods, and ended at a creek bed. That was my place. I would lie in the grass, tilt my face to the sky, and smile at the moon. Sometimes, when the weather interfered, I would instead journal under the cover of the night in my bedroom. I would crouch in the back of my closet with a flashlight and lay out my insides on paper. Whether in the grass or my closet, this is where my dreams were born and where they played out in extravagant detail. I saw my future, my career, my family, and my friends. I foresaw success and freedom. Always freedom. I wonder if when she swings, she sees her future.

At sixteen, I dreamed of being a teacher, having my own

children, and leading a life overflowing with love and laughter. In my own preparation for heartache, in my moments of anxiety and overwhelm, I also dreamed of these things being tragically ripped from my grasp. Of being found a fraud. Unworthy. I wonder if she has those moments too.

At sixteen, my dreams were lavish and detailed. They were in the full, vibrant color of present reality. They were real, and they were what kept me putting one foot in front of the other every day. My friends back then would tell you it was around this time I entered a bit of a dark stage. I couldn't articulate why I felt the way I did any more than I could fight my way out of it. There were days I would walk around carrying an inner ball of rage and looking for outlets in everyone I encountered. Picking fights. Being righteous in my grievances. I had hate and hurt and rage that needed a place to go, and high school had fertile soil. There were days I would wake up and put on the same clothes I wore the day before and walk as light and small as I could. I would leave class to hide in the bathroom. I would feel the cloud over me grow heavier and darker, but rather than fight against it, I'd wear it like a blanket, a cloak.

I didn't make active choices on any of those days, at least not that I remember. The only decisions I remember ever making back then were the ones that kept me from going home. I got a job and started working as many hours as school would allow and then agreed to get paid under the table for any hours over that limit. I would jump at the chance to spend nights at friends' houses then consistently feel nauseous when I arrived.

My life, my heart, and my whole body felt constantly in conflict, like there was a push-pull inside of me, and I never knew which side I was truly on or which I was rooting for. I began drinking and dabbling in drugs with some of the quiet, moody kids on the periphery of my friend group. They looked dangerous and torn. They seemed to either understand the turmoil swirling inside of me or at least offer an escape from it.

Sometimes, for my birthday, I would have friends stay at my house. I would be so excited for them to arrive. I'd devise a plan for the whole evening. We would play games, eat pizza, laugh, and fall asleep late into the night. We would tell stories and share secrets. I can remember when it was my turn to share, I looked around the room to make sure it was just us, then told of times I would wake up and everyone in my house would be gone with no clue as to where. No note on the counter, no phone call. Parents and siblings gone. The house would be empty and dark. I would eat, watch TV, and wonder if they'd ever come back. Scared they would and scared they wouldn't.

Seared in my brain is the moment I recall, too, that as I share these stories, I'm still at my birthday party. I remember looking around the room and recognizing the moment my story took that uncomfortable turn—realizing I'd voiced thoughts meant for my journal. Yet still, the party would go on. I would hold my breath and stare at my hands until someone else broke the awkward silence with a funny story or even better, a haunting ghost story. Then the party would continue as if I'd never spoken, never released a little of the storm inside me. I would sigh with relief and jump back into party mode, smile the biggest and laugh the loudest.

The next day, my friends would leave, and they would take with them the laughter, the lightness, and the consuming fun that could swallow up a night. Behind, there was left tension and darkness. Where just the night before was a doting host with jokes, gifts, and free-flowing affection, now was a parent who took inventory of the things I'd said and done wrong, my behaviors that had caused embarrassment. I remember walking around my house, cleaning up the remnants of the night before, and feeling confused and lost, untrusting of my own experience. Later, I would find my spot on the grass and replay every moment before, during, and after my party. I would play it over and over again and try to see where I'd gone wrong. Where I'd faltered and how I'd do better the next time. I would live it all over again and feel it all for the first time.

There's an interesting phenomenon that happens to people who live with trauma where they don't make memories. They simply can't remember basic things that happened. I won't learn about this phenomenon until many years later. For every year until then, from about age sixteen to age forty, I'll joke about my horrible memory. With my husband and kids, we'll all take to calling it a *Mom*ory. It's just a weakness, a fault, something in all my attempts to improve that I cannot. It's a failure that I'll wear as a badge as if to own it rather than letting it own me.

When I look back to my childhood, my memories have a hazy quality that I don't trust. The only thing that sticks is what I'm able to replay and etch for myself in the quiet moments I find later in the grass or in the dark of my closet. In my journal, I loved to write fiction. I wrote dark stories with brooding characters and twisty plots. Nestled between those stories was my life, the memories I was creating and recording. The thoughts that swirled in my brain needed a place to land, and I needed a place to put them so I could rest and they could make sense. In the pencil lead in my spiral notebook, there lived a girl who was real and had friends and a family. She existed in a way that didn't feel so solidified in my body and mind.

These are the last pictures I have of that girl, of me. My life went on, and it has been full and vibrant, busy and loud. I got married at twenty-two and had five children by thirty. I threw myself into motherhood the only way I knew how. I lost myself. My name was "wife of" and "mom of" for twenty years. I loved it. I thrived in the chaos and busyness of it all. The drop-offs and pickups. The soccer practices, dance lessons, and neighborhood playdates. I made lists to stay organized. I checked boxes. I smiled and waved at neighbors. I had date nights with my husband and movie nights with our kids. I put one foot in front of the other every day. My friends back then would tell you I was happy and my family was happy.

I have pictures from those days. I have random memories, though not many, not enough. Hence my *Mom*ory being born. I could tell you where to find misplaced soccer cleats, library books, and winter hats. I couldn't tell you what we did for my kids' birthdays, what those movie nights looked like, or how often my husband and I had a date night. I couldn't tell you what I believed in or supported, what I'd fight for, or where I'd compromise. I didn't have a lush green backyard to lie in. I stopped journaling. I told myself I didn't have time for those childish things.

In 2020, my husband and I divorced, and I moved to my own house. A house with 120 years of history. Somewhere over the last twenty-five years, I learned to love old houses, to appreciate their imperfections, to find my own home in the memories created before I arrived. Many years before, my husband and I had built our own home. I spent many nights sitting with him trying to explain why it felt cold. Yes, it was our home. We filled it with children, cats, and dogs. There were scratches on the walls and stains on the carpet. There were school pictures framed on shelves and kid drawings on the fridge. We hosted parties and celebrated dozens of birthdays and holidays with family and friends. There were many memories made there. They just weren't mine, and I couldn't find the connection. I was sure there was something wrong with me. It wouldn't be the first nor the last time I would be described as cold and contained.

I sit now in my old home, and I recognize why I've always been drawn to historic places, why I find my peace walking through antique shops and cemeteries. I feel like I've lived a life of forty-five years without leaving a footprint or making a memory. No indelible proof that I've been here or touched anything. That new home built from fresh wood and finished with fresh paint was an empty shell waiting for someone to fill it with energy and laughter, with pain and anguish, with love and moments. My new old house already has those things. There is no pressure on me to add to it, to fill a role, or to check more boxes. I don't need to worry about creating a home that looks and feels too much like that of my childhood. I can sit here and feel the lives of those who made a home here before me. I can feel their warmth and their memories. I found a home I didn't have to create from scratch. I found peace where someone else's story left off, and I found the freedom to pick up from there and add my parts, my moments.

It was in my late thirties when I learned that growing up in a home with a borderline parent would make so many of those struggles make sense. That walking lightly through life comes from a place of fear and unstable ground. It was in my forties that I realized I'd filled my life with to-do lists and plans, with expectations of myself and those around me, with rigid rules, explanations, and beliefs so I could create stability and safety. I knew when I had stability and safety, I could finally be me. I would be able to look back at sixteen-year-old me and tell her it was all okay. She could dream again. She could create. She could love and be loved. It would be safe for her to come out again.

When unpacking in my new old home, I happened upon a picture of myself as a young girl, arm in arm with a friend, smiling with my whole face. It was a smile and a face I hadn't seen in a very long time.

Sweetheart, you will smile like that again. You will live and you will love. You will have incredible children and be surrounded by friends and colleagues who respect and care for you.

You're a teacher, and it's just as amazing as you dreamed it would be. You are whole. You are kind. You are strong and capable. You are creating a life to be proud of. You are creating a life of love and laughter, and even pain and anguish. You are learning to balance, to be present, to sit with it, and to feel it all. You don't dream in a yard of lush green grass anymore, but you do journal again. You make those memories in the moment, and they're amazing and difficult and irreplaceable. You look in your new old backyard and see your youngest daughter, now sixteen, swinging in a hammock, singing along to whatever's playing through her headphones, tilting her face to the sky, and dreaming.

Life is neither predictable nor terribly consistent, but it's real and it's safe. It's stable and secure. You're home, and every minute of your journey back has been worth it.

ABOUT APRIL DAVIDSON

April Davidson is an American Sign Language/English interpreter and interpreter educator. She has a bachelor's degree in sign language interpreting and is working toward her master's degree in interpreting pedagogy. April is the mother of five children and two fur babies. She prides herself on learning and growing through every experience life offers. While life has been a series of challenges, April believes that if you can take something with you from each step of your journey, you will be well equipped for each new adventure. She loves to travel alone and with friends or family all across the country. There's little she'll say no to if it promises adventure, excitement, and new places to see and people to meet.

April is an introvert who thrives in the company of friends and inspiring people. With some time alone to read, listen to music, and journal, she'll be recharged and ready to take off on the next great caper in no time. When not hiking across the country or cheering on her kids from a soccer sideline, she enjoys running and dabbling in numerous DIY projects in her 120-year-old home.

To connect with April

april.a.davidson@gmail.com

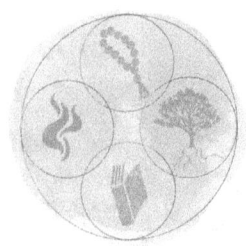

READY TO LAND, COMING HOME TO ME

Christina Mantel, MA

Standing in my childhood home, in front of my childhood mirror, I see myself and reflect on my past. I see images of myself as a young child playing with Barbies, and then I am ten, getting ready for school in my school uniform. I flash forward to an image of myself as a teenager, experimenting with makeup for the first time, singing into a hairbrush to ABBA's "Dancing Queen," dreaming of a future full of love, laughter, romance, and happiness. And today, decades later, I see my present self with wrinkles of time around my eyes. These are reflections of my life, and I think back to you, my younger self. You were so innocent, so full of excitement with big dreams of what you wanted in life. You wanted to be loved, to be safe. You wanted to be a mother. You wanted a large family full of laughter and connection. The future was yours, and anything was possible. You had dreams, and growing up, you steadily moved toward them. I am here to reflect with you on how life brought many happy experiences mixed with sad ones and some very painful moments.

A lifetime of experiences, and now time to embrace and reconnect with you, my younger self. Snapshots of my life flash in front of me: Parents proud of my academic achievements at my graduation from high school and UC Berkeley. At twenty-three, sparkling with joy while living in Paris feeling fully alive and thriving, thrilled with a view of the Eiffel Tower from my bedroom window creating a lifelong passion for France.

I danced, I laughed, I met incredible friends, and all my life I have had an incredible bond with my brother. I fell in love a few times; in the long run, I ended up married to the man of my dreams. I met him over twenty-five years ago on a random street corner in San Francisco while looking for a cab, which we then shared. We had the wedding of our dreams with my father walking me down the aisle and a memorable mother-daughter dance. As a couple, we planned on having children and starting a family; the future was so promising. My hopes for motherhood never died—until that day . . .

"There is no heartbeat," the doctor said to me, looking up from the ultrasound.

My heart stopped at that moment. Silence. "Are you sure?" That was the fifth time I had heard those words. Five pregnancies. Five heartbeats heard that had stopped. Zero babies taken home. With each pregnancy, there had been renewed hope, and with each miscarriage, utter sadness and grief. Each baby was special although my fifth pregnancy stands out. This baby was nicknamed Bruiser for all the bruises on my belly from the IVF procedure and injections of blood thinning medication.

I really thought Bruiser would make it. But there was no more heartbeat.

This day, one that started out with excitement, ended with devastation. I collapsed with tears flowing for the loss of my babies and my future. My hopes of becoming a mother were flatlined. My life shattered; this was the final straw. After years of trying to achieve something that for many women came so easily, was not to be for me. I felt broken—falling into a tunnel of darkness and depression. I became numb, it was as if time had stopped.

I was too fragile, unable to attend others' joyful family events, especially baby showers and children's birthday parties. My pain was a raw wound that would have salt poured into it by simple things such as a TV commercial showing happy families and children. This wound never healed into a scar; it remained open and festered. How do you pretend to be okay when your whole world and focus has been about becoming a mother and that has been denied? I withdrew and went into isolation. The acceptance of not having my own child evaded me and would haunt me for years—and is still something I struggle with today.

In the many years of infertility, I lost touch with myself. Determined to be a mother, I had the focus, the drive, the doctors, the hope, and all that was left was the pain. I felt like I was a failure as a woman. We were unable to adopt, and my inability to be a mother became a ball and chain that I did not realize was to follow me and drag me down as I got older. The pain did not fade over time; acceptance of my reality was blocked by my anger at God, who I believed showed me heartbeats and then took them all away. I had been a good girl and yet still had so much trauma in my life. What had I done—or rather who had I been—to have "deserved" so much pain and heartbreak? I paused to reflect about *you*, my younger self, and your influence on my life and how in many ways your unfulfilled dreams were haunting me and holding me back from living my life and having dreams for my life moving forward.

I look in the mirror, and I see a tear on my cheek as the pain is still there. As a younger child, I always thought I could achieve anything. Then I have an "aha" moment, and I say to myself, "These are not my younger self's dreams; these were her expectations. It was her expectation to become a mother." My stomach drops. In a moment of clarity, I realize she is still holding me hostage with her expectations and is not letting me go. I recognize the tension from this tug of war I am having with myself. I have not been able to move on from the pain of not fulfilling her expectations.

I needed to retrace my own steps, go back, and give myself permission to feel, to see what I saw, and to regain the parts of me that were left behind. "Younger self, I need to make peace with you, gain your forgiveness and your acceptance."

As a first-generation American, born to a German mother and Dutch father, your first language was German. In a classroom as a young child, other kids would tease you, calling you Nazi and Kraut. That left scars and pain around your heritage. You tried desperately to fit in. Navigating a new world for your immigrant parents, you were very responsible from an early age. You would often fill out school notes for yourself and your brother having your parents sign them as their first language was not English. As a child growing up in an alcoholic home, it was chaotic. There were fights, tears, drama, and unpredictability. And you often thought it was your fault. I can tell you now, it was not your fault.

Pops, the alcoholic, was a merchant marine who would be gone for months at a time. But when he was home, life was full of laughter. He yodeled when he took you to school, and all the kids came to see him. He looked like Elvis with his slicked-back dark hair and blue eyes. Pops was charismatic but inconsistent: he said he loved you often but from afar. Mutti (German for *mother*) was beautiful, a hard worker, disciplined, responsible, strict, and devoted to you and your brother. She represented safety. She gave you everything she could. You loved her with all your heart, but she was full of worry and smiled little. As a child, you believed it was your job to make her happy. This was an uphill battle and often one that made you feel like a failure. You tried your best to please her, but I want you to know that making her happy was not your job.

My younger self, you had huge fears of abandonment and of being alone. To escape the tension at home with arguments, raised voices, and slamming doors, you would often hide in your room. You spent hours imagining what a "normal" family was like and dreaming about your future and how you were going to make a difference in this world. You also had magical thoughts of being rescued and that if you waited long enough, things would get better. You had to believe that to make it through those unsettling times. You had to create a safe place in your mind—a place you had power and control over.

Looking back, I realize these are some childhood fantasies and coping strategies that you set up so you could survive. Catholic school taught you to follow the "rules" that you thought would keep you safe. If you were a good girl, got good grades, and did not cause trouble, that would guarantee rewards. To a child's mind, that made sense. You believed it was like an equation. If you behaved a certain way, your wishes would come true; life would compensate you in a positive way. To a certain extent, it was like thinking of God as Santa Claus: he would give you everything you want, if you are good and not naughty.

Back to the mirror. I look in my eyes today, and I am ashamed that I haven't fulfilled my younger self's expectations. Angry. Stuck in the anger. The hope I was given with each pregnancy was brutally taken away. I was in the waiting room of my life, not wanting to accept that time was passing, still holding on to a chance my dream could happen, and reality would just disappear. I was still grieving a wound that never healed. All my attempts to avoid my truth, by staying frozen, did not free me. None of my hopes that something or someone else would rescue me ever happened. Believing that if I did not accept the outcome, I could control the uncontrollable, was magical thinking. Unfortunately, despite what I believed, doing everything right and being the "good girl" still did not guarantee me a happily-ever-after.

I have this image of me in a plane, circling an airport. I am circling and circling in the fog with no clear direction or destination. I don't know where to land because I haven't decided where I am going next. I remembered all the plane trips to various destinations in my life. Where I was ready with my bags packed, excited to go on a trip, I knew where I was going, and had plans of what I was going to do when I landed. However, somehow on this trip, while in the air, my destination disappeared. Motherhood was no longer on the map, nor was the dream of a large family as my parents were now gone also. So, I continued to circle with no dream of a new destination. I was in a plane with nowhere to land.

It dawned on me that not deciding is a decision. I am attached to being stuck and circling, and perhaps attached even to the suffering. *I am preventing myself from having new dreams and becoming vulnerable again to avoid more pain, hurt, and disappointment.* Although unhappy, I have become desensitized to time passing on and opportunities passing me by.

Slowly, I unraveled my process and discovered the story I attached to my experience was stopping me from moving forward. There was the fact and then the fiction, and they were different. The fiction was the story I had believed for so long that it had become my truth. Could I be wrong? Could I give myself credit for having tried to have children and release this self-punishment? Could this be possible? Resistance to reality is what has caused my suffering and kept me stuck in my underlying grief. Someone once told me, "Surrendering to reality does not mean you have to like it." *Can I give up my need to control? Am I willing to surrender?*

I cannot press fast-forward or rewind; I need to live in this moment. I need to forgive myself for where I am in my life's journey and accept my reality. I want to release myself from the versions of myself I have created just to survive. I want to stop the chapters of pain and rewrite my story to one of empowerment and freedom. A novel thought. A seed of hope is planted, and to be honest, I don't remember the last time I felt hope. I sense a shift, and it feels like there is a crack in the armor around my hardened heart. I breathe a sigh of relief.

A flash of a memory pops into my mind, tinged with excitement, as I remember when I jumped out of a plane with the word "FREEDOM" written on my hands. I recall the exhilaration of exiting the plane door, fearful but bold. The rush of the wind, the astonishment that I had jumped, the thrill of the fall with the view of the beautiful California coastline, and then, after the parachute opens, the serenity of the slower descent. I found the courage to jump, and I had survived. Savoring this example, I realized that I could have the courage to change and move forward. I started to think of embarking on a healing journey to freedom and re-finding and perhaps even reinventing myself. This time, destination: me, a destination of self-love and hope.

I return to the mirror, and I remember something my father once wrote:

> "Learn to enjoy your own company.
> You are the one person you can count on
> living with for the rest of your life."

If I want a future self who is not hurting, I cannot get to this future self without letting go of the pain from the past. I realize I need to make a *you*-turn, or rather a *me*-turn, and reach out to my younger self and make peace.

I look deeply into my eyes and say to myself, "I see you, my younger self. I am sorry, I really tried, but I feel like I failed you. Please forgive me. Let me go and move on and rejoin my life and come up with new dreams for our future self. I love you and always have. I wanted to make you proud, and I still do. There is a hole in my heart that will never be filled, but not accepting reality is not working for me anymore. I will not abandon you. Let me take your hand and walk forward into our future, and know that I am here to protect you and I want to hear you cheering me on. We are safe. We are okay. I want to invite you into my heart, and I will bring you with me wherever we go. I just wanted you to know."

While I had waited and hoped to be saved by a hero, it became clear to me that I needed to be my own hero. I needed to be a "Mero" for my present self, my younger self, and my future self. It is time for me to have the courage to change course and discover my way forward. It is about self-evolution and the journey of "landing" back into my life with new dreams and aspirations as I learn to feel again. The thawing of my frozen self has begun. I am coming out of the fog of numbness. Perhaps circling in this plane has been a cocoon for me all along and it is time to break free and spread my wings.

I hear a noise, the Fasten Your Seatbelt light turns on, and the plane starts its descent.

I cannot help but smile. I hug myself and feel a pulse. I have a heartbeat.

I am *Ready to Land* back into my life.

I am coming Home to Me.

ABOUT CHRISTINA MANTEL, MA

Christina Mantel is passionate about empowering women to get unstuck so they can land into their life and have freedom to choose next steps. She advocates for those who struggle with the integration of their past traumas and grief. Developing a healthy mindset requires self-love and the willingness to accept what you cannot change. Separating fact from fiction and removing the story you attach to reality can be liberating. She promotes the goal of being your own "Mero," evolving into the heroine of your own life story.

Christina is an honors graduate of UC Berkeley with a master's degree in clinical psychology. She has worked in the mental health profession for over twenty years, coached women with ADHD, and counseled callers on a suicide prevention hotline. Currently program manager in the Department of Psychiatry and Behavioral Sciences at the University of California, San Francisco (UCSF), she is known for being strategic with strengths of empathy, communication, networking, and advocacy. She is co-chair of the Diversity Communications Committee and a member of the Women of UCSF Committee.

Christina is a first-generation American and speaks German, French, and English fluently. She is the podcast host of *Ready to Land*.

To connect with Christina

www.ChristinaMantel.com

BROKEN TO BEAUTIFUL

Alaria Taylor

"'For I know the plans I have for you,' declares the LORD, 'plans to prosper you and not to harm you, plans to give you hope and a future.'"

—Jer. 29:11 NIV

I had a traumatic childhood. Then a very traumatic period between the ages of seventeen and twenty-three. Those combined events almost destroyed me, but I came out the other side stronger.

Many fairy tales have an evil stepmother who tries to kill her stepdaughter. As a child, I identified with Sleeping Beauty and Cinderella and used to cry myself to sleep after watching those childhood movies, wondering if my mother might actually be my stepmother. Why did she hit me and strangle me? Why didn't she like me? What did I do wrong?

She said, "Don't ever have children, they ruin your life" hundreds of times throughout my life. The message was clear: She believed I ruined her life. She lashed out in anger and beat me, choked me, punched me too many times to count. She broke my braces, broke my nose, tore my eardrum, and when she took me to the doctor, she always instructed me: "Tell them you fell down." I dutifully obeyed. My grandmother (dad's mom) told me, "Your mother ruined your father's life by getting pregnant. He was dating Miss Florida!" I often felt like I shouldn't have even been born.

My mother's favorite way to abuse me was to throw me on the bed, straddle me, then strangle me, repeatedly thrusting down with her hands around my throat. Years later, when dating my future husband who was in chiropractic school, he took X-rays of me to complete some of his clinical requirements. He was stunned to see that I had a reverse cervical curve in my neck. My mother repeatedly thrusting down on the front of my throat hundreds, probably thousands, of times actually changed the structure of my neck. After receiving gentle chiropractic care from my husband for many years, he completely corrected that.

I did have some fun and happiness during my first three years of high school. I signed up for just about everything I could to get away from home. I was a cheerleader, in the class play, president of the Pep Club; I sang in choir and solo ensemble contests, in the musical, in swing choir; I had lots of friends and a steady boyfriend; and I attended all the dances. School was a wonderful escape from home.

Then something horrible happened. During spring break my junior year, I was raped. An acquaintance refused to give me a ride home and insisted her friend drive me instead. I'm still not sure if she set me up intentionally. I was stunned. Afterward, I wasn't myself and couldn't shake it off. I couldn't smile or laugh anymore. I kept staring off into space. My boyfriend of three years kept asking me what was wrong. I couldn't tell him I was raped. I was afraid he would break up with me. Every day he'd ask, "What's wrong? Are you mad at me?" I'd say, "No, I'm not mad at you." He'd ask, "Then why are you acting like this?" I'd say, "I don't know."

And I didn't know.

I wrote in my journal, "This should not still be affecting you.

It happened over a week ago!" I can actually laugh about that now, decades later. Little did I know. Within weeks, we broke up because of this. Then a bad situation became worse. His friends wrongly assumed I dumped him and spread rumors that I cheated on him. They were yelling at me in the hall at school, calling me a whore and threatening me. An expletive-laden note stuffed in my locker promised to kill me. My parents' mailbox was firebombed and destroyed. This wasn't bullying. It was terrorism. I lost my boyfriend and almost all my friends. I was shell-shocked and devastated . . . and now I was suicidal.

I had been an A student, but my grades plummeted. I frequently skipped classes, went to the nurse's office, laid on a cot, and cried. I felt all alone, believed I was damaged goods, and I feared anyone finding out the truth.

Two months later, in an attempt to cheer myself up, I went on a date with a guy from another school. This was only the second guy I had ever dated. He drugged me, drove to a deserted location, dragged me out of the car into a field under the expressway, and sexually assaulted me. My jeans had buttons on the side instead of the front, and he couldn't see very well because it was nighttime. No matter how hard he tried, he was unable to get my jeans off. Otherwise, I would've been raped again. I gained ten pounds in one week after this assault without eating differently. I later learned that extreme stress can make the thyroid shut down.

One year later, after high school graduation, I was raped again, this time by a guy I had known since fourth grade. I was furious, screaming at God with tears streaming down my face. "Why are you doing this to me? What did I do wrong? What did I do wrong?" I felt like Jenny in the movie *Forrest Gump* when she collapsed on the ground, throwing stones at the house where she was abused. I did not report any of these assaults to the police because back then, victims were attacked on the stand, and I knew I would never survive that.

I made a lot of vows that night. I vowed never to return to my hometown. I vowed no one would ever see me again. I wanted to get far, far away and never think about any of this again. I hated everyone and everything, including myself. I was going away to college to start a new life and forget everything.

I was broken in a million pieces, and I didn't know how to put myself together again. People who knew me had no idea because I covered all of this pain with sarcastic humor. There was a cartoon character, Daffy Duck, who would occasionally get blown up causing all his feathers to come off. He'd walk around picking up all his feathers one by one saying, "Fortunately, I keep my feathers numbered for just such an occasion." I could relate to that. Part of me was trying to find the humor and the other part was thinking about suicide every day.

Incredibly, the list of horrible events does not end here. During my freshman year in college, my dorm room burned down the week before final exams; a professor lost my final exam and gave me an F for the course, claiming I never took the exam; I broke my ankle while registering for second semester, and my adviser told me to quit school. I refused. I was hit by a car my sophomore year in college. That summer, a young girl was brutally raped and murdered two blocks from my apartment. Two weeks later, police arrested the driver of the car I was in for drunk driving and sent me home with a man on a motorcycle, who I assumed was an off-duty police officer. He was not. He could very well have been the murderer in that case that has still never been solved. The story of what happened to me that night was on the front page of the campus newspaper.

When I was twenty, I swallowed an entire bottle of Valium, locked my bedroom door, and laid down to die. I wasn't upset or crying. I was at peace with my decision. I didn't write a note. I just couldn't take any more pain. Within minutes, someone was knocking at my apartment door. I ignored it. Then they started pounding on my door. A guy I had recently met in my college show choir, who had never been to my apartment, was out there, and he would not stop. He was yelling, "You're not going to believe what happened! I have to tell you this!"

As he continued banging on the door, he was shouting his funny story as loud as he could. I began laughing. That's what snapped me out of it. Laughing was still good. I got up, let him in the apartment. He brought ice cream. I took a few spoonfuls, then excused myself to throw up the pills. If he hadn't brought the ice cream, it would've been difficult or impossible to throw up all the pills. I believe God sent him.

When I was twenty-two, a roommate emptied my checking account by intercepting my ATM card and code in the mail. I had to secretly meet with the FBI multiple times before her arrest. When I was twenty-three, my car was stolen by a man who exactly matched the description of a serial rapist in my town. He abandoned my car but kept the keys to my apartment. All of these things happened in a very short period of time, one on top of the other. I was a nervous wreck and developed an eating disorder. I tried the best I could to just put everything out of my mind and carry on.

During these years, music was my escape. I threw myself into music, and that's where I allowed the unexpressed emotions to be expressed. I auditioned for a college show choir called the Wisconsin Singers. I never had a voice lesson or a dance lesson, but somehow, I made it competing against hundreds of other students. Being in this show brought me great joy and lifelong friends but also stress. I had a new boyfriend/fiancé from a different school, and everything was wonderful between us during the first year of our relationship—until I made this show. He didn't like it and did not want me to try out for the group the following year. By then, we had dated for two years and were engaged. When I told him I would be in the show for a second year, he threw his glass across the restaurant, breaking it, walked out, and left me there without a ride home. Another long-term relationship destroyed. I felt all alone in the world. I couldn't trust anyone, especially men. I threw myself into music even more.

I stayed in Wisconsin Singers for three years, then auditioned for and made the mainstage show at Marriot's Great America theme park, then four dinner theaters in Florida, then two cruise ships. Before *American Idol,* college kids that wanted to pursue singing tried out for theme parks, professional musical theater, and cruise ships. I was thrilled to have been selected for all these exciting, prestigious shows, but something was wrong. On the outside I was always joking around, but inside I felt damaged and depressed.

The Turnaround

How did I become a happy, healthy, successful person and not a ticking timebomb of insanity? Many things: music, maintaining my sense of humor, writing my thoughts and feelings in a journal, therapy, being relentless in the search for my purpose, forgiving everyone completely, finding my husband, and most importantly seeking God and praying to Him.

One night, sitting in a parking lot crying and talking to God, I asked Him to send me my husband. I didn't want to date anymore. I couldn't take any more painful, broken relationships, just send me my husband. Less than a year later, a guy from my high school walked up to me in a bar and started a conversation. Even though I vowed never to see anyone from my high school again, he was extremely sweet and kind that night, so I lowered my guard and let him in. We've been happily married for thirty-seven years. God had the perfect husband selected for me. One with a caregiver's heart and a calm temperament that wouldn't trigger my as-of-yet unresolved issues. My husband helped me heal. He is literally the answer to prayer.

One day, I came across an article about kintsugi, which is a type of Japanese pottery where they take broken ceramic pots and repair the cracks with gold. The finished product is stronger and more beautiful than the original unbroken piece. This is a beautiful metaphor and how I have decided to look at my life. The broken pieces can be put back together.

From the age of eight, I always had a diary or a journal and wrote in it regularly. I believe that helped me process these painful experiences. I had a place to vent, and writing things down helped to clarify my thoughts. I would alternate between talking to myself and talking to God in my journals.

I repeatedly wrote, "You are going to have a wonderful life. You are going to sing, write songs, travel all over, and you're going to have a wonderful husband who will love you." I didn't know anything about affirmations or the power of visualization at the time. Amazingly, all of those things came true. I have written and recorded my own music with a Grammy award-winning producer, won over fifty national and regional songwriting awards, and became a voting member of the Grammys. I performed on cruise ships, in theme parks, in coffee houses, in an opera company, with the Milwaukee Symphony, in rock bands at *Summerfest: The World's Biggest Music Festival*, and more. I am a Jack Canfield Success Coach and the director of Chick Singer Night Milwaukee. Recently, I coauthored a best-selling book. And I'm not done.

I was relentless in my pursuit of healing and my pursuit of God. I received a bachelor's degree in psychology and a graduate degree in spiritual counseling and comparative religion. I studied spiritual formation in another graduate school program. I read hundreds of books on self-help, theology, healing, prayer, and spirituality. In my thirties, I finally went to therapy for eight and a half years until my psychologist finally said, "You should really be five hundred pounds and in an institution, but you're the most sane patient in my practice. Why is that?" I just pointed up and replied, "God."

I am completely cured. Thank you, God.

I learned that forgiveness is an important key to healing— the purpose being to remove the bitterness from my own system, rather than excuse the bad behavior of others. I forgave the men who raped me. I learned that my mother had her own long list of horrible events, and I was able to understand and forgive her completely. We had a wonderful, loving, normal relationship the last eight years of her life. The still, small voice of the Holy Spirit guided me to the right books, courses, and a psychologist who specialized in exactly what I needed. The same voice of the Holy Spirit spoke to me when I was journaling, telling me what a wonderful future I was going to have. That same Holy Spirit helped me write award-winning songs and is the source behind all my creativity. These experiences have inspired many of my original songs, including "Nobody Else Like You." The link to the video is in my author bio.

You think it's over, you think you're all alone
You grab the bottle, and disconnect the phone
There's Nobody Else Like You, there'll never be again . . .
God don't make mistakes. It's no accident you're here.
Hold on tight. It's not too late.
Your purpose, your purpose will be clear.

I know what it is like to be broken. I know what it's like to feel permanently damaged beyond repair. If I could go back and speak to my younger self, I would tell her: "Hang on, hold on, God didn't make a mistake, you are supposed to be here. God has a plan and a purpose for your life, and that purpose will be clear soon. Keep praying, keep talking to God, keep writing in your journal. This is just a short season of your life. You will overcome and heal, and you will have a beautiful life despite these events. No one gets through this life unscathed, but that does not mean the rest of your life is destroyed. You will be happy again, have a wonderful life, help others, and rise from the ashes of this despair. Don't give up!"

If you are reading this book right now, then you are supposed to be here on Earth at this moment. In all of human history, there has never been anyone exactly like you. You are here for a reason. Even if your parents didn't want you, God wanted you and wants you to be here. He has a purpose and a plan for your life. Do you know what your purpose is? Make it your mission to find out. His thoughts are not our thoughts, and His ways are not our ways.

I used to ask, "Why did this happen to me? Does God hate me?" Now I know that God never hated me and He is not the author of evil.

Instead, I ask, "What good came from this? Did God take me off one path and put me on another? What is my purpose in life and how did these events prepare me to fulfill it?" When I first thought about writing to my younger self, I wanted to warn her so she could avoid these horrible events: "Watch out," "Don't get in that car," etc. But then I realized I wouldn't be the same person. Those years of despair made me search relentlessly for answers, for the meaning to life, for healing, for God, and for my purpose.

I am most definitely a different person because of the things that happened to me. I believe I am a better person. I have empathy for others going through horrible situations. I understand the power of forgiveness. I have a deep desire to help others. I have researched and studied so much in an effort to help myself that I can now use that knowledge to help others. I understand how music can help heal a shattered heart and how singing can help heal a voice afraid to make a sound. I know what it's like to be broken. And like kintsugi pottery, I know what it's like to be put back together and be stronger and more beautiful than before.

ABOUT ALARIA TAYLOR

Alaria Taylor is a certified Jack Canfield Success Coach with degrees in psychology and counseling and over thirty-six years managing a holistic healthcare clinic. As an award-winning singer-songwriter with over fifty national and regional awards including voting member of the Grammys, she has performed on cruise ships, in dinner theaters, with rock bands at *Summerfest: The World's Biggest Music Festival*, in performances and interviews on television and radio, and much more. She is an international best-selling author and director of Chick Singer Night Milwaukee.

Her passion is assisting others in fulfilling their dreams and overcoming obstacles to success both personally and professionally. She is a certified vocal coach for both speakers and singers with special training in trauma-informed vocal coaching.

As a certified Canfield Success Coach, virtual facilitator, and methodology trainer, she coaches groups and individuals to discover and achieve their goals and unlock the keys to their success. She can customize a presentation or workshop for your organization. Additionally, she can work with you individually either in person or virtually, helping you get from where you are . . . to where you want to be.

To connect with Alaria

www.alariataylorconsulting.com
www.alariataylor.com/consulting
Music video: "Nobody Else Like You"

UNSAFE

Christina Allison

The first time I visited my younger self, I found myself as a small girl around the age of two or three. I was looking out the front glass window. So many emotions flowed through me: fear, confusion, sadness. I knew I did not fully understand my feelings, but something was wrong. Why was the babysitter that was supposed to be watching and protecting my brother and me, the one hurting us? This was not the only incident in my life where I was physically, sexually, and emotionally abused. My story, at times, horrifies people. Some people ask me how I was able to hold on to my sanity through it all. Now that I have entered my fifty-ninth year around the sun, I can articulate how I became the person I am today in ways my younger self couldn't.

I learned early on that the world was not safe. Those that should have been there to take care of me or protect me were also my abusers. I cannot recall ever feeling truly safe growing up. I did not understand the significance of this at the time, and I have wept for the little girl I was. This became the thread that connected the first three decades of my life. As a young adult, I believed no one would like me for me, let alone love me. I always saw myself as having to be sexual to be loved. This belief does not make for good or safe relationships. I lived a very unsafe and promiscuous life of my own making and surrounded myself with people doing the same. Unsafe was familiar and comfortable to me. I often contemplated how I would take my own life through these years; thankfully, I did not. I later recognized that I was very lucky that I avoided truly awful consequences to my life, and I feel someone, or something, was watching over me through the years.

I had only seen the world through a dark lens. When I met my husband, he introduced a new perspective. My husband has had sex with two women his whole life, and he married both of them. (Not at the same time.) He challenged my core belief that I could not trust men to be faithful to their spouses. I have seen many examples of cheating husbands, including those who cheated on their spouse with me, of which I am not proud. My husband opened my eyes to an entirely new perspective. He was faithful, and he loved me. I even remember a conversation about suicidal thoughts with him where he mentioned that he never had suicidal thoughts. This took me aback; I had never even considered that you could live that way. This was the actual start of opening me up to seeing another perspective. Cracks were starting to appear in the foundation my abusers had created.

The revelations and healing that came from having kids were something I was not expecting. It was hard to see myself through their ages. I would think, "I was just that age," "They are so little; how could anyone do that to a child?" As parents, we try to give our children a world without the bad things we endured, but we cannot control their life experiences. They will have their own unique traumas. None of us get out of this life without scars, but I wanted to ensure that my children did not have to see the world in the way I was unlearning. How do I teach them that the hard times are what make us who we are? I wanted to show them you can take an experience and decide what to do with it.

This meant I needed to be open and upfront about the healing I needed to do.

I started by surrounding myself with people who made me feel safe and loved. I created a family that keeps me safe and loved. I put a lot of time into learning about myself and others with the help of some fantastic (and some not-so-fantastic) therapists and coaches. It has taken a lot of work, and I am still far from perfect. We are all flawed, but we can choose how we will go forward.

This revelation was vital to my healing—it taught me the power of choice. I get to choose who I want to be and how I see others. I choose to see this world as a loving place with beautiful people in it. I want to see the good in everyone and understand that we are all learning about ourselves and others. I choose to see the world as a safe place. I had strongly tied my identity to the stories I believed about myself and the "unsafe" world I saw around me.

I have had many uncomfortable and difficult conversations this year in preparation for writing down my experiences. It has taken me decades to talk openly about the abuse that happened to me. We need to make people uncomfortable. I know many people who have survived abuse, and they deserve to have their voices heard. I deserve to have my voice heard. What I realized is that I am freer when I tell my story. I no longer feel shame or guilt that I am ruining someone's life by telling my story. The guilt and shame I had to hold on to when I was younger kept me feeling small. This process has allowed me to feel empathy for others and compassion for those who are abusers. What they did was not okay. I can forgive and understand in a way most people cannot. Forgiveness is not about the other person but an act of strength for yourself. Forgiveness means that you are not carrying the hurt, fear, and anger with you going forward. I know this to be true. I look at my abusers as the hurt people that they are. Something horrific must have happened to these people to do what they did to me. Knowing that they were hurt allows me to forgive and remember that they are people first. Hurt people will either hurt people or help people but above all they are still people.

It is now my mission to end the silence of sexual abuse. One in three people are survivors of sexual abuse, and I believe this number is much higher. This makes the silence surrounding it even more apparent; they are still considered taboo and uncomfortable topics. Silence often lasts longer than abuse. Survivors become the keeper of the secrets of others, and this burden is just another form of abuse. When even adults feel uncomfortable talking to other adults about abuse, how can we expect our children and young people to speak up? Let's discuss all abuse so we can all heal as survivors and abusers. People cannot do better before they know better. I wish to spread the relief I felt when I could finally share my story, to allow others to release the shame and guilt many have carried for far too long. No one deserves to feel unsafe in their lives. We often have more power in our thoughts and behaviors than we have allowed ourselves to believe. I chose to be safe and created that life for myself as an adult. I know that anyone can, and my passion and calling is to help others create that for themselves. The first step is sharing our stories. This stops the cycle of silence that leads to more abuse.

If you have survived abuse in any way, know that you did not deserve it or do anything to bring this onto yourself. I am so sorry that this happened to you. Know that you are not alone and that there are compassionate, safe people who want to help you become the person you were always meant to be. This was one of the hardest lessons to learn; to be open to good people who wish to help you. Your story is your own, and you can have difficult and uncomfortable conversations. There is nothing to be ashamed of; you did nothing wrong. Above all else, love yourself. These lessons are things that I wish I could share with my younger self staring out the window, but I am blessed to be able to share them with my children—hopefully contributing to making their world a safer place.

ABOUT CHRISTINA ALLISON

Christina Allison aims to be a compassionate major change agent in the lives of others. She is passionate about empowering others to reach their full potential. She has spent her life learning how to be a catalyst to the transformation in others. As a survivor of sexual abuse herself, she uses her story to inspire others to own their truth and end the silence surrounding abuse.

She is a lifelong learner with interests in learning about people and their behaviors. She has a bachelor's in organizational behavior and leadership from the University of San Francisco and a master's in communications from Queens University of Charlotte. She is also a Certified Professional Co-Active Coach from the Coach Institute and is a certified trainer for both the Canfield Training Group and Pryor Learning Solutions. She launched her professional company BFF Enterprises LLC in 2009 to help entrepreneurial women create the lives of their dreams.

Christina lives in North Carolina and is a wife and mother to two beautiful daughters. She loves spending time in her craft room and learning to make beautiful creations. She sees the world as a beautiful place and desires to make it even more beautiful.

To connect with Christina

www.bffenterprises.net

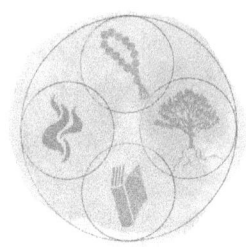

SILENCED BY A TOUCH

Pegie Brandt

"**W**hat do you mean I have to learn to forgive myself?!
I didn't do anything wrong!" I yelled at my
counselor.

I had been the victim; I was the one who was violently
attacked and raped at ten years old. I was also the one who was
drugged and woke up with a grown man, my neighbor, doing
things no one should do to a child! I was also the one who had
been beaten by someone I should have been able to trust. This
counselor, this woman, was wrong. She had no idea what I had
gone through. I stormed out of her office crying and yelling at
her. If I had to tell my younger self anything, it would be to go
back inside and really listen to her, not wait for years to revisit her
words and understand their meaning.

At eighteen, I had gone to counseling for another reason. I did
not want to repeat the mistakes of my stepmother. I wanted to
keep calm when I needed to discipline my son. I wanted to make
sure he was safe from me. I didn't want to even remember all the
physical pain I had endured most of my childhood even though
physical marks would stay with me, reminding me, forever.

I burst into the building holding my son of two and a half

years old, crying, and screaming, "I don't want to be like her, I don't want to be like her." That morning I had awoken to find my son painting circles, triangles, and squares on a final portrait that was sold and ready to be delivered so I could pay my rent. I was furious! I yelled at him and stormed into the bathroom, hitting and breaking the mirror, ripping down the shower curtain, punching an unforgiving wall—acting like a mad woman. When I finally calmed down, I exited the bathroom to see my son sitting across from the door crying and telling me he was sorry. I began to sob. I scooped him up and drove to New Day, a counseling facility just blocks from my house.

As I entered the building crying and stating that I didn't want to be like her, I had not realized that my son had chosen a burgundy red color to paint the circles, triangles, and squares on my painting. The crimson color was bright against his yellow footie PJs, resembling blood. Suddenly there were three people pulling us apart and taking my son away from me, into a separate room. After they learned that "No, Mommy didn't hit me, she just beat up the bathroom," we were united in front of a counselor.

For months, we concentrated on my childhood abuse, learning to stay calm whenever addressing discipline with my son. Putting on headphones and listening to smooth jazz before discussing what and why any bad behavior would not be allowed worked for me. My son to this day at forty-four will say he was lectured "forever," but I never struck out physically while upset or angry.

Later, what came out of my sessions eventually was the rape and the molestations I had endured as a child. I had never forgotten them, only buried them. I could not understand what this counselor was telling me I needed to do: allow my mind to forgive my body.

During our last session, she had asked me to put my arm out in front of me. She touched my arm. "What do you feel?" she asked. "Tell me you don't feel me touching your arm." I looked at her. "Yes, of course I feel it." Then she said something powerful, even though I denied it and became angry at her words.

"Your body," she said, "cannot lie. It will feel all physical things—cold, heat, pain, and yes, pleasure—even if your mind denies it, at least for a second. Even if it is experiencing horrible situations, it will respond to what is happening, sometimes finally shutting down from shock. Your body, in certain areas, will feel pleasure. It is time that you forgive your body for misunderstanding the touch that has silenced you. Once you forgive your body, your mind will heal." This had been a powerful message—one that I wish I had listened to immediately.

Unfortunately, I was too angry, yelling and leaving her office, never to see her again. I waited years to revisit her words. Those words and my action of forgiving my own body allowed me to accept and recover. I actually can sit in the same room as my rapist and love him for the soul he is today without anger, hurt, pain, or any other negative feelings. I have shared this with several women over the years, and each one reacted similar to how I did. Some of them sought me out later to thank me. To this day, I wish I could find that counselor and thank her too.

ABOUT PEGIE BRANDT

Pegie Brandt was born an artist. Her doodles were far beyond that of her older siblings. As she aged and became educated in the arts, she was told by the artist Wyland that she is an artist and finally started to believe it herself. Her friends of thirty to fifty years old have called her a chameleon, constantly changing. Experiencing new things was easy for Pegie. Coming from a military family that constantly moved helped develop this side of her.

She was a mother at the age of sixteen and still believes it was the best thing that ever happened to her. She's grateful for her son every day. Married, enjoying a loving relationship with a strong, handsome, and caring man.

She was one of the first female police officers in the 1980s in Redlands, California. She bought her first home when she was only sixteen and had her first rental property in her early twenties. She was a licensed realtor in two states over a period of ten years as a second or third source of income. She is still investing today along with property management—constantly working two or three industries at once. She was a retail manager for a large department store, was educated in construction design and interior design, and became a CEO and co-owner of a wireless construction company at the beginning of the industry from the eighties until 9/11, which forced the closing of their company.

After that, she became a music and art academy owner of three locations and taught art, which she learned more about as she taught. Recently, she closed the academies at the start of the COVID pandemic after receiving the state letter to stop all face-to-face education. Now, while still performing real estate investing and construction design, she is finally becoming an author with the help of Kate Butler and her team.

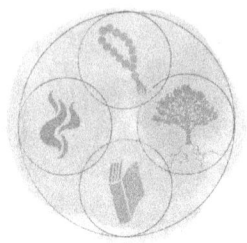

I SEE YOU AND LOVE YOU DEEPLY

Donna Nudel Brown

Oh dear Donna, as our sixtieth birthday is quickly approaching, I have been thinking a lot about you. Mostly how you managed your way through those challenging years of middle school and high school. If you only knew then what I know now, you would see how amazing you are! You would see how everything that makes up *you* is such a gift. You would see how the pieces of you that were different and unique as well as the pieces that you didn't like about yourself are in fact what makes you extraordinary! I want you to know that I see you, I thank you, and I love you with my whole heart.

You will eventually see how all those times you felt like you didn't fit in would ultimately shape you into who you are now. Those experiences allowed you to become a compassionate, sensitive, empathetic soul, a great listener, and a caring, loving, loyal, thoughtful friend.

We all have lessons to learn in life, and you mastered so many of them.

All those times you felt left out and isolated ultimately led you to tapping into your creative, soulful spirit.

When you felt excluded, you relied on your imagination and

used visualization to see yourself in a different light. You mastered this skill long before it knowingly became a tool for creating your future. Your quirkiness, your viewpoint, your curiosity, your understanding of how people interact, react, speak, and intertwine with others made you the incredible observer that you are.

At a very young age, you learned to identify when people were being authentic and genuine and truly cared; and you were also able to discern when they were not.

Those teenage years were the toughest for you, and I want you to know how much I thank you and appreciate you and say, "Well done!" I know there were so many moments when you felt isolated, alone, and excluded, and you wondered how you would make it through that time. I still feel some of your pain, and I know you often didn't feel seen.

Know that *I* see you, and I am so proud of you!

You developed coping skills far earlier than most because you required it for self-preservation. I know those formative years were painful when you felt like you didn't fit in or belong. I know how uncomfortable you felt being overweight and even more uncomfortable being teased about it. I see you and feel your discomfort all these years later.

The biggest gift you received was your sense of humor. Thankfully, you learned to lean into humor as your coping mechanism—knowing that if you could make someone laugh or distract them, it would ease your discomfort. Who knew, nearly forty years later you would use that gift by standing on stage performing stand-up comedy!

All those times you felt bullied, you learned to appreciate your true friends even more. Just so you know, you will still be very close with two of them when you are sixty. I'm sure you can't even conceive of being sixty at your age! It is actually pretty cool and looks a whole lot different than it did in 1978!

I know you often felt like an outsider looking in and became an observer out of necessity. You were able to read people's body language and always knew when their body movements did not match the words they were speaking. You knew when they were posturing for attention and now realize they were merely trying to hide the parts of themselves they didn't like.

As an observer, you decided how you wanted to be and show up. You sometimes tried to be like others and quickly realized how uncomfortable that was and learned what did not resonate or feel right to you at the time. You will be glad to know as an adult, you learned what aligns and what does not align with you. Of course, we did not have this vocabulary at your age, but our body always knew. It took a long while for me to trust my instincts. I *so* wanted to fit in, and I often ignored those instincts. I eventually learned to trust myself, but it most certainly wasn't easy.

Trust has always been a tough one for us—at your age and even now! I have been hurt and betrayed and left out and embarrassed in every phase of my life. You and I are *so* sensitive. Honestly, it has been challenging being this sensitive. I felt it then and continue to feel it now; our tears have always flowed easily, and we learned early on that it makes others uncomfortable. I can now honestly say that I *do* trust myself after doing the deep, inner work. I have connected with others who have my best interest at heart. I was finally able to exhale and share my inner thoughts knowing they would be held close and safe. I learned that wisdom and trust come from experience, growth, and time. That insight took decades.

I wonder what your classmates who teased you all those years ago would say if they could see you now. Just look at you! Did you ever imagine you would be standing on a stage with incredible women who see the light in you? Women who seek your guidance and viewpoint? Women who invite *you* to speak to their audiences to teach and support them? Women who want *you* to sit at their table and ask you to share your expertise? I didn't, and I do it even when I'm scared.

As recently as ten years ago, you were still hiding in plain sight. What I am doing now was never part of our imagination. There were no thoughts or visions of achieving any of these amazing accomplishments. In fact, you will use all the lessons and knowledge you have learned over the years to heal and support and guide others through *their* challenges. How incredible is that!

We have had so many experiences—some were fun and exciting, some were filled with fear, and some were lonely and painful. When you went to college and were excited to be on your own, you were seeking all new experiences, many of them pushed your boundaries. My favorite was the time you jumped out of an airplane—it was wild! I am so proud you did that even though it was terrifying and thrilling. I still laugh as I recall the memory of you needing to be rescued from the tree where your parachute was tangled! Your bravery and those images were with me the day I leaped from a cliff.

About your education . . . the crystal ball shows you going to college—actually, three different schools—but ultimately there was another path for you, and you left without graduating. Even though you will struggle with that choice for a long time, you will finally come to terms with it because you made the best decision for yourself at the time. You genuinely believed your decision to leave college before graduating meant that you were not smart. It turns out, smart doesn't only come with a college degree. It comes from experience, understanding, absorbing, observing, compassion, curiosity, integration, and interaction with others. And while you may not be able to solve physics problems, there are so many talents and skills and knowledge you have that override and supersede the notion that informs how smart and wise you actually are.

Perhaps you are wondering why it was the best decision to leave college. Well, you made choices that ultimately led you to meeting your future husband and the father of your three children. I know as a teenager, that is so, so hard to comprehend!

When you broke up with your high school boyfriend, you thought it was the end of the world and could barely see past the pain. I'm sure you remember all of those times you wondered if you would ever find someone who loved and accepted you for exactly who you were.

You couldn't possibly imagine that you would marry a kind, generous, adventurous man who loves you unconditionally. You meet him when you are twenty-five, and you will get married when you are thirty. The irony is that you meet him while working in a restaurant and you would likely not have met him had you graduated from college with the degree you were initially seeking. You will be blessed with three amazing children who are kind and generous and funny and smart. They are *so smart!*

You never know what surprises are in store for you when you choose a different path. Always be open to any and all possibilities. It's okay to have a plan, and it's also okay to know when that plan is no longer the right path for you, and you desire to pivot. It's so important to be true to yourself and honor your heart and your spirit. We all have our own unique gifts and blueprint, and we must find the best fit for us.

Please know, all those painful memories and experiences will prepare you for this incredible life you will be living.

There were so many times you doubted yourself, when you didn't feel like you belonged or fit in, when you were self-conscious of your appearance, and when you were afraid to speak up and share how you really felt. I'm so proud of you for finally finding your courage to honor yourself, to be true to yourself, to speak your truths, and to follow your intuition even though you had no idea how you were guided. Now, we won't mention some of your questionable choices, even though many of them are giggle worthy—but I also know you learned so much from the missteps and the poor judgment you sometimes showed.

Ultimately, you listened to your heart and followed your path even though you weren't sure where it would lead. You eventually found your purpose after doing the deep inner healing work and now guide others through *their* challenges, allowing them to find their purpose and inner calm. The irony of it all: your life experiences led you to doing what you love.

I know it looks like everyone else has confidence, a clear direction, bodies they love and are proud of, and everything they desire. I want you to know, I believe we all have struggles. They may not be visible, but I believe we all have something we would love to shift within ourselves. It may be something small or completely life changing. We never know what others are facing, and they often don a mask to seem like all is well. We all have our unique path and develop coping mechanisms. What I want you to know is that we are all on our own unique journey.

I encourage you to always surround yourself with friends who lift you up when you need it, who listen when you crave an honest connection, and belly laugh with you at the absurd. It may be the same person who can do it all or a handful of incredibly special people. You deserve to be surrounded by friends who love you unconditionally. I have found my people, and it feels amazing to know I have friends I can always call when I need them. I can't imagine my life without them!

My point, dear Donna, is that we can look at others and assume they are deliriously happy, that their life is perfect, and they have no concerns. What I know now as I approach turning sixty, is that not one single person's life is perfect. We all have concerns and worries and doubts, and face experiences we never ever considered, such as health challenges or the sudden loss of a loved one or a natural disaster. I know life as a teenager was complicated. I also know you will be well equipped to handle anything that comes your way because you are *so* strong. You are resilient, you are beautiful inside and out, you are fiercely loyal, you are an amazing friend, you are incredibly resourceful, you will become a loving wife and mother, and you love with all your heart.

You are also deeply loved.

And if you can imagine this, you will raise incredible children who are wise and generous and become incredible adults because you and their father raised them with love and compassion. Well done, you!

I know you are often hard on yourself for all the times you made poor choices or decisions that led you down a path you didn't anticipate. The times you felt unlovable were incredibly challenging. I see you so clearly and feel your heart. I want you to know that each of your decisions ultimately led you to finding joy.

I want to thank you, young Donna, for making all those choices—crazy as they were at the time! I so love your adventurous spirit, and you will be happy to know I still have it. You will show yourself how brave you are when you jump off a cliff at age fifty-one! I know, it strikes *me* as incredible and awe-inspiring!

I did it to avoid adding another regret to my list, and it completely changed my life! I was definitely thinking of you when I leaped. In fact, *you* were my inspiration. Each time I recall that memory, I think of you and say, "We did it!"

Always be true to yourself, always listen to yourself, and tap into your intuition and listen to your body for clues. Our bodies have the answers and will guide us intuitively if we are open to receiving the messages.

I keep reminding myself how brave I am, and I thank *you* for that. I look at you and recall how amazing and brave you were to travel through Europe *by yourself* when you were twenty! You truly amaze me! I think of those times, and it allows me to tap into my bravery.

We did well, Donna! Thank you for showing me what bravery looks like. Thank you for showing me what enjoying life looks like. Thank you for showing me what it looks like when we stop caring what other people think of us. Thank you for showing me how important it is to find what makes us happy and to surround ourselves with people who make us laugh and cry (goodness knows we do plenty of both).

Thank you for all the life lessons and teaching me it is okay to be me just as I am and know that I don't have to be like anyone else. Thank you for teaching me how important it is to honor myself completely. The only person who must love what I think or do or how I show up is me. Some may see that as selfish; I see that as honoring myself. We only get one shot at this, so let's make it the best it can possibly be. Continue to be amazing, continue to be curious, continue to be brave, continue to laugh and find the humor in every situation, and continue to love with all your might.

I want you to know when you are my age, you will have learned to accept yourself and love yourself just as you are. You will be true to yourself and only do what aligns with you and not because someone else is doing it. You will have the courage to step way out of your comfort zone and be seen for exactly who you are. And because of you, I am ready to be seen. I can honestly say, I fully and completely love myself.

Enjoy the sunsets and moonrises and take as many photos as your heart desires; there are so many people who love when you share such beauty. Be sure to enjoy Mother Nature as much as possible; it will fill your heart and soul. Continue to be the light for others so they know they are not alone.

I love you with all my heart.

Keep shining your bright light!

Love,

Almost sixty-year-old Donna
xoxox

ABOUT DONNA NUDEL BROWN

Donna is an intuitive energy coach, Reiki Master and teacher, inspiring speaker, crystal expert, and #1 international best-selling author. Donna guides women who have put their own dreams on the back burner while taking care of everyone else and are now ready to focus on themselves. Together they dust off their dreams, align them with who they are currently, uncover and discover what the next chapter looks like, and create the path to fulfillment and joy. She often supports empty nesters as she knows the space quite well.

Donna shares the energy of Reiki and crystals with her clients who often experience clarity, focus, insight, and a sense of calm. Donna is grateful for her ability to support and guide others on their journey and is especially grateful she is able to do so remotely.

Using her pendulum, Donna selects the exact right crystals for her clients. Her pendulum also assists them in seeking answers to life's tough questions, allowing them to follow their path to find joy.

Donna is excited to see how her life will continue to unfold and evolve in the most amazing way. She is open to any and all possibilities and continues to say yes to all that aligns with her vision, her passion, and her purpose.

To connect with Donna

www.DonnaBrownDesigns.com
Donna@DonnaBrownDesigns.com
Instagram: @crystals_to_clarity
Facebook group: Leap Into Fabulous
LinkedIn: Donna Nudel Brown
Linktr.ee: Donna.Brown.Designs

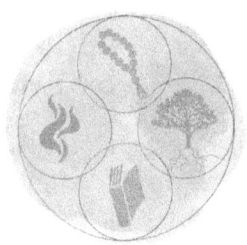

HOW GOOD IT GETS

Stefanie Caley

Hello, gorgeous! Wow. Here I am on the precipice of forty years old, and I have been given the opportunity to tell you all the things I wish I knew when I was younger. There are so many things I want to tell my younger self. I mean, I could tell her things that might break the rules of time travel and urge her to buy as much stock as she can afford in Microsoft and Apple. Honestly though, as thrilling as it would be to make her wildly wealthy and set her up for an easy life, I'd be doing her a disservice because although she will come upon many obstacles and hardships, they will enrich her life in ways she cannot yet foresee.

You may be wondering, *What do I desire to tell you sweet, young, naïve girl?* So much so that I hardly know where to begin. Settle in and get comfy. I have so much to share, in no particular order.

Never let anyone tell you that you are too much or not enough. Neither is true nor accurate. You are a vibrant, radiant, beautiful human with so much love to give and gifts to share! Remember to always give that love to yourself first. When you love and accept yourself, everything is possible and no one has the power to override your own knowing of that. There are many people in this world who will try to convince you that you are too talkative, that you shine too bright, that you cannot possibly be so happy all the time, that you are not tall enough, not smart enough, and on and on. You know who you are. Let all these judgments flow off your back. Their opinions don't matter, and I guarantee you, those who truly know you and love you will never speak to you this way.

You will go on to do a plethora of things like earning your bachelor's and master's degrees. Things you dreamt of, yet honestly weren't certain you had the stamina or intelligence for. You will work part-time and full-time jobs while going through college, and you will oftentimes feel resentful of those whose parents pay for their education. You will come to understand that some of your best friends are made through these jobs, and your character will be strengthened by having to balance it all. When you reach your master's level studies, you will unfortunately have to take on massive debt to finish. It is overwhelming when you think about it. However, the good news is, because of that program, you will meet a friend who introduces you to your husband, and your life will be forever changed in the best way because of this introduction, making every sleepless night of studying and all the work worth it.

You will work in medicine with your degree for some years, but oh, beautiful lady, just you wait because your true calling hits you like a ton of bricks when you become a Mama! I wasn't planning to spoil the surprise for you, but I can't help it. You're going to have kids. Two of them! The journey of becoming a Mom will be agonizing at first. You'll lose your first pregnancy and you'll question whether your body can carry to full term. You'll wonder if you did something wrong. Then you will finally come to the knowing that the universe has a plan for you, and this is all part of it.

When you become pregnant again, you'll worry about every little thing, and I know you never thought you'd have any children or even find a man worth having them with for that matter. Believe me when I say you will never feel more joy than becoming a Mom. Ahem, uhh . . . and you will never feel more triggered, frustrated, annoyed or angry as when your kids become a mirror for you or learn to press all of your buttons! You will have healing to do. It's okay. You do heal. And you are such a great Mom.

The best part of being a Mom is getting to see the world through their eyes. Things you find mundane or expected, your kids will bring new life to. Traveling, although more difficult in some ways, becomes more exciting for seeing it from their perspective.

As I was saying before about your true calling: you will become an entrepreneur in order to better serve new Moms in a way that feels aligned for you and them. At first you will doubt your ability to be as good a coach as some of the seasoned social media influencers, but let me assure you that the Mamas who choose you have life-changing results, and you will never feel surer that what you do matters and that you are making the impact you were always meant to.

You will help Moms all over the country and world step into Motherhood with more knowledge of their choices, support through the overwhelm, and endless questions of things they didn't know they did not know. You will remove the shame, guilt, and fear around miscarriage, trouble with breastfeeding, making the right choices for their families, dealing with overbearing family members and friends, sleep issues, post-partum blues, and a ton of other topics. Moms will spread the word to their friends who are expecting that you are the real deal, and before you know it, your business is thriving and your heart is beyond overflowing with gratitude and fulfillment. Can you believe how good life gets?

The remainder of this letter to you are all the random nuggets of advice that I desire you to have. May they serve you well and keep you well on your path.

If you haven't gathered by now, the basis of life is about

having experiences, making memories, and choosing who you make those memories with. It's about following your heart, creating your joy, and making the most of what the universe gives you.

Choose your friends wisely. Don't waste your time or energy on anyone not matching your vibration or raising it. Stay focused on being kind, marching toward your desires, and listening to your intuition because ignoring it has unfortunate consequences. And remember, don't give anyone permission to walk through your mind with dirty shoes.[1]

Never be afraid to love people with all your heart. It doesn't always mean their love will be reciprocated, but know that you will never regret giving love. Your love, in fact, may drastically alter the trajectory of someone's life for the better. It is too much of a gift to hold back.

Don't be afraid to ask questions. How will you ever learn if you don't ask? And the answer will always be no if you don't ask. I cannot tell you the number of times you will ask a question someone else was scared to for fear of judgment, embarrassment, or the like, and when you ask, it relieves them of that pressure and enlightens them too. Knowledge is power. Gain as much as possible. It is something no one can ever take from you.

Get out of your comfort zone. The world is an amazing place, and the vast majority of people in it are good. You will never know that for yourself unless you step outside of what you are familiar with. The more you challenge yourself to be bold and take calculated risks, the more alive you will feel.

Make a bucket list while you're young, and take every opportunity to cross something off the list. You don't know how much time you have in this life, so never take it for granted.

Experience anything and everything you dream of. Don't be concerned with the expense of traveling (there are ways to do it on a budget), of creating opportunity for the experiences you want to have. You can and will always make more money. I'm not saying you shouldn't save. A smart youth starts planning for the future. Having said that, any money that isn't being stashed away for retirement or current bills should be invested into living your life right now!

Trust me, in the moment, you'll feel nuts for spending a couple thousand hard-earned dollars on a weeklong trip, but years from now, you'll cherish the memories and be so incredibly glad you made it happen!

Do more and worry less! Don't look back on your life one day and wish you had heeded my advice.

Travel like mad for it will expand your horizons beyond measure and make you realize that we are all more alike than we are different. Go to all the outings your friends invite you to. Look, I know you're a self-proclaimed ambivert, but when you push yourself to be more active in your friend's lives, the bonds you will create last forever. That is priceless. Seize all the opportunities you can possibly fit into your days (while still getting adequate sleep, of course!).

Another thing, love: quit putting off life's adventures to finish school or find your life partner. You will get through school if you desire to. A chance to whisk away to Jamaica or Sedona for an epic weekend or a friend's wedding will not present itself twice.

As you know from what I already mentioned earlier, you will find your partner. It may seem like forever you've been waiting to meet your best friend and start a life making memories together, but trust me when I say that all the things you're doing and all the choices you're making are turning you into the perfect person for your spouse. It can feel heart-wrenching to watch your friends find their soulmates. You are happy for them always, but it would feel so nice to have that for yourself. Hear me out though. If you met him at twenty, it wouldn't have worked. You were too immature then and had growing to do. Don't put your life on hold . . . for anything! Keep growing, changing, and enjoying the moments. Your future self depends on it.

Besides, you and your spouse will have so much time to make

new memories together. It is simply another chapter in your life that you get to write! Speaking of which, marriage changes things. Not for better or worse (yes, pun intended), but it simply makes things different. You will make joint decisions that affect both of you. Decisions about where to live, what car to drive, when and where to spend money, whether to have children, and so on. The pace of your life will change. Things you used to care about won't be as important. Priorities shift. Embrace this.

When you get older, you'll reflect back on your childhood, your teens, twenties, thirties, and you will feel such immense gratitude for all the beauty in your world.

The people who guided you and in some way shaped you into the magnificent being you are. Even those who made your life hell in the moment. You will be able to see the lesson in them crossing your path. How you needed the experience they brought in order to gain wisdom you needed later. They may have also needed you to teach them a lesson. Remember how I said earlier that giving love to others may change their life's trajectory for the better? Yeah, love. You are that powerful! More obviously, the people who brought joy, laughter, love, and light into your world. Gosh, what a wonderful blessing to have people who go through life alongside you. People who will support you in myriad ways and support all you do. You will often reflect on the fact that you are fortunate to have more loyal and amazing friends than maybe any one person deserves!

I realize I have thrown a lot at you to absorb in this love note from the future. Truth be told, I could probably go on for much longer. However, I am going to take a deep breath and share one last bit to carry you through your days. There are a lot of things that don't make sense to you as you move through life. You'll sometimes feel like you wasted your time, money, or effort on something or someone. Please believe me when I tell you none of it is a waste. Without the mistakes made, the hard times, the moments of feeling stuck or lost, you wouldn't find your resilience, you wouldn't know true joy, you wouldn't come to realize that you always have options and that you always knew the way. The contrast is what allows you to be grateful, to recognize all the good, all the lessons. As you look back, you will see how each move you made drew you closer to where you needed to be. It will all become clear, and it will all make sense. Oh, sweet girl, keep your head held high. This life is happening for you, and you have far more control over it than you are sometimes led to believe. You deserve all the beauty, light, and love in the world. I love you. All of you.

Note: *You may have noticed that I always capitalize the words Mom, Motherhood, Mama, etc. This is done intentionally because it is my belief that Moms are deserving of distinction and that Mom is a proper noun. It is our name, our title.*

1—"I will not let anyone walk through my mind with dirty feet," Mahatma Ghandi according to Goodreads Quotes, Goodreads.com, accessed February 3, 2023, https://www.goodreads.com/quotes/2450-i-will-not-let-anyone-walk-through-my-mind-with.

ABOUT STEFANIE CALEY

Stefanie Caley is a Motherhood mentor and coach for new Moms, a professional photographer, and a nationally board-certified physician assistant. She is also a devoted Mama of two, a Reiki practitioner, and an avid lover of travel.

As a mentor to new Moms, Stefanie guides her clients through Motherhood with a nonjudgmental, unbiased, loving approach. Having a medical degree, researching consistently, and being a Mom herself provides her with a vast array of wisdom and experience, which she uses to support her clients to build their confidence as a parent and release the overwhelm and stress that often comes with transitioning into Motherhood.

Stefanie's loved ones, colleagues, and clients describe her as compassionate, loving, insightful, and heart centered.

When she is not mentoring Mamas, Stefanie can be found outdoors with her own children or lost in the moment with her camera.

Stefanie's other interests include health and wellness, studying the human body and mind, manifestation, quantum physics, and learning random or obscure facts.

To connect with Stefanie

YourMamaMentor.com
YourMamaMentor@gmail.com
Instagram: @YourMamaMentor
Facebook: Your Mama Mentor
Private Facebook Group for Moms: Free, Fearless and Fulfilled Moms
YouTube: @YourMamaMentor
TikTok: @your_mama_mentor

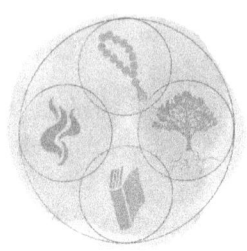

INNER GUIDANCE

Jacquie Freeman

When I was a little girl in the 1960s, we lived a half block from the elementary school. Walking home each day across the path that many people walked, I'd play a game of finding treasures. As a child, it felt magical and I felt guided to look in certain spots along the gravel and sand path. From turquoise rocks, and shiny quarters, to tiger's eye marbles, and pretty barrettes, it was seemingly a magical walk home. The other kids would ask me how I always found things and I'd tell them I just expected to find these little treasures! I was not often disappointed. That ability to look for and expect to see treasures, and for life to feel magical, has served me well my entire life.

I graduated from college with a degree in elementary education. An opportunity appeared for me in 1980 to use my degree when a teaching position was advertised in my local newspaper. The school year had started two weeks prior, and Jackson Elementary needed an additional teacher for an overflow of kindergarten students. I was excited when I received the call I was hired and would be starting the following Monday. The other five kindergarten teachers had each selected seven students from their crowded rooms to give me. By the end of my very first week, after a particularly bad morning, I sat forlorn at my desk while my class was at recess.

The thirty-five five-year-olds in my class seemed out of control, unruly, and angry and seemed to have little academic skills to do the worksheets the other teachers had given me to hand out. (The other teachers gave them all the same work and had told me to do the same.) I was overwhelmed with all the problems and felt in shock with how bad the class was!

What have I gotten myself into? I wondered. I burst into tears and lowered my head to my desk so no one could see me. Feeling overwhelmed, I wondered how I could quit. Then an inner voice came to me, "Look for the treasure in each child!" Something about the voice jolted me, and I sat up and thought, *There has to be a good kid in here somewhere*! So resolutely, I picked up my pencil, brushed away my tears, and began to search my mind. It took a moment, but I began to write. By the time I was done, I had jotted down the following names: Charity, Jeffrey, Ricky, Marlena, Diana, Amy, and Frank. I had come up with seven names out of the thirty-five, but that was all. These seven children were well behaved, academically doing well, and very pleasant children. I smiled to myself. *There* are *some good kids in here!* Then I noticed something very important that I had not noticed previously. I knew which teachers had given me which students, and I saw that all seven of these children had come from one teacher, Mrs. M. She had taught at the school for decades. I had already noticed how well her students behaved that first week compared to the other classes and how she spoke softly to them and they minded. That afternoon when I thanked Mrs. M for giving me these students, she told me something I have never forgotten: "We each had to give you seven of our students. I knew which seven students the other teachers were going to give you. I decided to give you my very best!" No wonder my class seemed unruly. The other teachers had sand-bagged me giving me their very worst students!

Mrs. M had given me a gift in many ways, and I began to

look for what I wanted to see in each child. Her kindness helped me begin to see my class in a different way. The seven students that were already a delight became excellent role models and helpers. I established fair and firm rules, natural consequences, and abundant rewards. I found something positive each day in each student. I instilled pride and respect into my classroom. The students felt nurtured and before long they were showing each other love and respect. I developed academic groups for students that adhered to what they already knew and threw away the standard lessons I was supposed to give to everyone and met each student where they were. I put in the time and attention to raise each group academically and with good self-esteem.

I also ran parenting groups to help the students as this was a big factor in why some of the students had been misbehaving. Before long I had a classroom with thirty-five wonderful children. It seemed almost magical when the behaviors that I was looking for and wanting appeared within a few weeks! Parents began wanting their children in my classroom, there was such a difference!

My principal noticed, and she suggested I consider obtaining my master's degree in school administration. She thought I'd make a wonderful principal. I did want to start my master's degree, but not in administration. What I had seen in my students had interested me in learning more about self-esteem and discipline. I decided I would obtain my master's degree in counseling and become a school counselor. I would have to go part-time, and it would require me driving two hours to most of the classes on campus after working all day. The more I looked at the requirements, the more I knew this two-year program would take at least three years to complete. I was reluctant to sign up and get started, and I kept putting it off. It just seemed too difficult.

The semester was about to start up again when I pushed the application aside and once again thought, *This master's is going to take too many years to finish.* That was when my inner voice strongly said, "The years are going to go by either way, and you'll either have something to show for it or you won't!" I recognized this inner guidance system of mine! This inner guidance has helped me my entire life! The words reverberated inside me, and they made sense. I decided to fill out the application and quit putting things off. It did take me three years to finish my master's, but the very week I finished was also the very week the school counselor at my school site took maternity leave. Without so much as an interview, my principal asked me if I would take over her position. I began my school counseling career, a career that changed the trajectory of my life.

I loved being a school counselor and helping students and parents. I created many innovative and award-winning student programs. I won leadership awards, became one of only seven mentor teachers for my entire school district that employed over three thousand five hundred teachers. I loved what I was doing.

Dear younger self: Keep loving what you're doing. That passion is what makes it easy for you to go above and beyond!

At one point, the district superintendent asked me to write a grant that would help bring in money to help at-risk elementary students. It was a learning curve, for sure, but I wrote with the method that had always served me well: I looked for the treasure I wanted to find at the end: *What was the grant wanting to accomplish? How could I get there?* I obtained that first grant, and it brought in millions of dollars. I established a program at three elementary schools. After that success, I was asked to write more grants.

Eventually I was moved up to a school district position and was writing grants and overseeing my programs at thirteen elementary sites. After nine years, I had written twenty-two grants, received twenty-one of those grants, and had brought in enough money to employ over thirty-five people at those elementary schools. We helped nearly ten thousand students receive services because of those grants! However, I missed being on-site and working with the students myself. I enjoyed supervising the people in my programs, but I wanted to work with the students and parents myself! I also made a substantial increase in pay because of the work I was doing. I felt torn. *Dear younger self: It's never been about the money. It's the passion I have for what I do.* I consoled myself that I wasn't *that* unhappy. So I put a request in to my Higher Power. I'd always received guidance that moved me in the right direction. When I'm living my most aligned life and listening to my inner guidance, things always work out.

One afternoon, as I prepared to leave for the weekend, a flyer for a new elementary school program caught my attention. I quickly perused it. The focus of the new program was to help all of the retained students throughout our large district who were going into fifth grade. The district would bus all these previously retained students to this school to focus intensely on their academics and behavior. As I quickly looked the flyer over, I saw they were going to make use of the old Air Force School that had sat vacant for years after the base transitioned to a reserve base. The entire project sounded exciting. The flyer also announced upcoming interviews for reading specialists, psychologists, counselors, and teachers. I tacked the flyer up on my peg board; I wanted to keep an eye on this school's progress.

Back to work on Monday morning, my office looked just as I'd left it, except for one thing. The flyer that had been tacked up on the peg board had fallen onto the floor. I tacked it back up, but it kept falling off! It was then that I noticed the bold writing on the flyer that read, *Interviews for counselors to be held in room I-3,* and the date was that very day and the time was exactly right then! Since I oversaw programs at thirteen elementary sties, I wondered which counselors might be interviewing, and since the room I-3 was next door, I decided I'd walk past it and look for myself. As I walked nonchalantly by the room, the door was wide open. Trish, a friend of mine, on the interview panel saw me and exuberantly said, "Jacquie, get in here! I want to introduce you to Mark Yohonn!" At first, I could only see the back of this young man's blond head, and I thought he might be interviewing for the counselor position.

Trish continued, "Mark's the new principal at Arnold Heights!" Mark had a beaming smile. We shook hands and had an instant rapport.

Trish explained, "Our first appointment didn't show up, and if you have a minute, we'd love to pick your brain about the new school and the counselor position. Have you heard about the new program?" Mark and I immediately began lobbing creative ideas back and forth between us like a championship game at Wimbledon. Mark would mention varying goals, and I'd suggest dozens of things that I thought the new counseling program could offer to reach those goals. Trish, Mark, and I were having a ball, and before we knew it, nearly thirty minutes had flown by. We noticed that the next appointment was now waiting outside the door. We quickly wrapped things up and I excused myself. I walked back into my office delighted with the new principal and the prospects for their exciting new school.

The next morning when I came into my office, the message light on my office telephone was blinking. No cell phones in those days, so the message was waiting for me on the landline. I picked up and listened. It was Trish, my friend who had greeted me the day before. "Jacquie, I know you weren't interviewing yesterday, but Mark wants you to be the new counselor! We interviewed a lot of good candidates, but he loved your ideas and your vision for the school. I'm sure you weren't expecting this, but if you want the position, it's yours. Call me back as soon as you get this message."

I sat there stunned. I hadn't considered this for a moment, at least not consciously. There was no way I could leave my current position to take the Arnold Heights position. I picked up the phone and called Trish back to clear up any confusion.

"Trish, I wasn't interviewing! I was just sharing ideas yesterday."

"I know," she said, "but Mark loved your ideas and felt you

shared the same vision. We have a back-up person just in case, but honestly, no one else came close. What do you say?!"

"Louise would kill me if I left! Who could take over my programs? It would take weeks to train someone new!" and I heard myself starting to concede just a bit.

"We can give you some time to train someone to take your place."

"I couldn't possibly," I stammered.

"Well, make up your mind soon. We need to submit the name today!" and she hung up.

I now sat feeling unsettled but less stunned than before. My mind started thinking of the ways it just might possibly work. Could I train someone to take my place writing grants and training at my thirteen sites? I recalled there'd been a school psychologist that recently had asked me about how she could learn to write grants. I could train her. Then I thought about the pay situation. I'd be making a substantial amount less, probably $15,000 less per year! I couldn't walk away from that . . . or could I?! I realized I felt excited about the possibility placed in front of me to work with students.

I smiled looking at the flyer still on my desk and thought about it falling repeatedly off the peg board. I knew what I had to do. I walked next door and knocked on my boss's door. "Louise, we need to talk . . ." and I closed the door behind me.

Dear younger self: Take the job! Forget about the money! You're in for a great ride!

Those years at the old Air Force School were some of the best of my entire career! I loved working with Mark and the other teachers and specialists. They'd truly hired the very best. We raised students' academics three or four years in the span of only ten months! I created a TV and radio show and highlighted students on a local channel. I created leadership programs for the students and created parenting programs that parents could be bussed to each week. We made huge improvements, and I loved it! I saw treasures in each of these beautiful children, and I got them to see their own treasured lives and the possibilities that were before them!

Near the beginning of the second year, Mark accepted a position at the County Office of Education. I knew it couldn't have been an easy decision for him to make. I hated to have him leave, but I supported him and his decision. Mark said he'd always be around if we needed him and promised to come back to visit.

"I'm going to hold you to that!" I said, giving him a big hug.

"Keep changing people's lives!" were his parting words to me. Those words made my heart happy, and I knew we all would band together to continue his vision.

Our new principal was also a first-time principal. He was an incredible educator and leader and did a seamless job taking over. One rainy morning, he approached me very solemnly and said he had to talk to me in private. He was choked up, and I could tell he was about to tell me something very serious.

He said, "I just got a phone call. Something terrible has happened." I braced myself and listened intently without saying a thing. "There's been an accident." I sat motionless, intent on each word. "Mark was driving home from a county seminar. A drunk driver crossed two double lines. He hit Mark's car head-on. Mark didn't make it."

I was devastated. We all were devastated. One of the brightest lights I'd ever known was gone. It was hard to believe. We all seemed to help each other through it. I helped the students, staff, and parents; and the students and parents helped all of us.

Near the end of the third year, we received some disheartening news. We were informed that our school would be closing. The district would no longer fund the school, and the old school was going to be demolished. We'd all been through so much together. We were making dramatic and transformational impacts on lives. How could this happen?! The Success Academy had been pivotal in the lives of children and their families. It had changed lives, as Mark had once told me that I did.

On the last day of school, I experienced something I won't ever forget. As the students were saying goodbye and getting on their school buses to leave for the last time, a sudden wind kicked up.

Many of the students began pointing up above us excitedly shouting, "Look at the birds! Look at the birds!" Above our heads, we saw beautiful white birds circling us. There were at least ten of them! Where in the world had they come from? They soared above us almost ceremoniously. They were beautiful and looked like white doves to me.

As we watched in awe, I felt a sudden shiver go up and down my spine, and one of the fifth-grade teachers said what some of us were already thinking: "Feels like Mark's here with us." It was a very special moment.

As the buses left the school, the gusty wind stopped. It became quiet. We stood silently, many of us in tears. Then we watched as what had appeared as beautiful white doves, just moments before, surprisingly began slowly floating down to the ground. They weren't birds. What we saw now, without the wind in them, were simply white, plastic, grocery bags. They landed right in front of our eyes! I was glad I had experienced this treasured moment that made me feel Mark's presence as we said goodbye to the students of our success academy!

After retiring at the age of fifty-five in 2009, I was far from done. I am a Reiki Master, a meditation master, mandala artist and author of an award-winning book, *Daily Rituals.* I still find treasures inside each person I work with. I host empowering retreats in beautiful places where my clients experience their own hidden treasures hidden deep inside of them. I love creating and organizing beautiful yoga and Reiki retreats and giving Reiki classes and other spiritual workshops.

Dear younger self: Keep listening to your inner guidance, and keep helping others find their most magical and purposeful life by listening to theirs.

ABOUT JACQUIE FREEMAN

Jacquie loves to teach and create powerful offerings to help people live their most soulful and successful lives! Jacquie has hosted over eighteen Empowerment and Reiki Retreats in beautiful locations such as Sedona, Laguna Beach, Lake Arrowhead, and Carlsbad.

Jacquie is a Jack Canfield Certified Trainer of the Success Principles, a Reiki Master, Reiki Master Level Instructor, sacred mandala artist, certified yoga teacher, oracle reader, sound healer, and the author of the award-winning book, *Daily Rituals – 30 Days to Peace, Empowerment and Clarity*. Her classes, retreats, masterminds, and Reiki apprenticeships weave in listening to your inner guidance along with success principles, wisdom, spirituality, and humor. She is a lifelong learner, a manifesting queen, and credits living a joy-filled life to her daily practices of meditation, prayer, inner guidance, gratitude, and to the example of her mother and father.

Jacquie holds an MA in Counseling, a BA in Education and is currently working on her PhD in Metaphysical Science. Jacquie was selected as Counselor of the Year for the state of California by the CSCA in 1997.

Jacquie and her husband, Vernon, make their home in Southern California, along with their rescued Siberian Huskies.

To connect with Jacquie

https://www.meetup.com/reiki4u
https://www.DailyRitualsToday.com
https://www.JacquieFreemanReiki.com

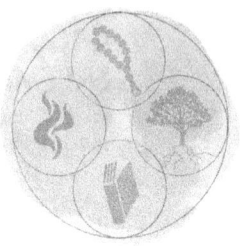

LITTLE MISS INDEPENDENT

Kristine N. McQuown

"No one can make you feel inferior without your consent."

—Eleanor Roosevelt

Being a single parent is tough. It's something I had in common with my mom at one point in my life. I grew up in New Hampshire, and when I was four, my parents got divorced. My tiny world changed in an instant. My dad was gone, and my mom started working three jobs to support us—Chagnon's Florist, K-Mart, and a shoe shop. I was the baby of the family. Laurie was ten years older, and Donna, five. During this transition, they became my babysitters, and I longed for my mom.

After our house was sold, we moved into an apartment. I had to leave the only home I'd ever known. I remember it was especially hard to leave my swing set, as the tiny yard I was about to inherit did not have one. Over the next few years, I settled into what was my new life. Kids are resilient that way, and I was no exception. I made friends, liked my new school, and there was a little family-owned store that sat two houses down from us on the corner. I'm pretty sure Short-Stop Market was the inception of my sweet tooth!

Meanwhile, I had an aunt and uncle who lived in Michigan. They both worked at a union factory, making good money, and receiving good benefits. Two things my mom didn't have. Although she would have to leave her home and the rest of her family, the decision had been made. We moved to Michigan three weeks before my ninth birthday. More change and another new school. Heck, a new state! Far away from everything I knew.

I remember the door to our apartment on Wilson Street being propped open with a heavy antique iron. There was a piece of bright-orange posterboard with two holes punched at the top, burlap string running through them. The sign read, *MOVING SALE,* written in thick black marker, and it was hanging from the hook that usually held our wreath at Christmastime.

I also remember going to the post office with my mom later that week to ship my aunt and uncle our fourteen boxes. Fourteen. Everything else was gone.

I started the fourth grade shortly after we arrived in Michigan. We lived with my aunt, uncle, and five of my cousins for six months until my mom had saved enough money and found a place for us. It was on the opposite side of town, so that meant a transfer to yet another school.

As my mom slowly began furnishing our small apartment, I began exploring our neighborhood on my new bike. There were several kids my age, and everyone I met was fascinated with my New England accent.

I can hear them now . . . "Say *pop*!" "Say *car*!"

Having low seniority, my mom had to work second shift. Three thirty to midnight, Monday through Friday. Laurie had decided to stay in New Hampshire with her boyfriend. They would eventually make the move to Michigan, but until then, it was just me and Donna from the time we got home from school until we went to bed at night. Weekends were the best because my mom was home. We would pack a lunch and go to the park or watch a funny movie. She had a great laugh, a wicked sense of

235

humor, and she loved licorice! Our movie nights always included licorice.

I have no idea if it was because she trusted us, but we didn't have any rules. There were, however, expectations:

1. Wash any dishes that you dirty.

2. Leave the house the way you found it.

3. Take the trash to the curb on trash night.

No mention of a curfew or doing homework. No mention of keeping the door locked. Just those three things. And so began my journey to independence.

My mom was lucky that I was a good girl, and a bit of a chicken. I was shy and not keen on trying new things.

I liked routine, I liked rules, and I liked to play it safe.

I *did* leave the house the way I found it, and my homework was always done as well.

I liked going to bed early. That way I could fantasize about my "perfect life" as I drifted off to sleep. Having two parents, a dad who came home every evening in a suit and tie: his briefcase hanging by his side. We went to Hawaii and found a cursed tiki necklace, just like the Brady's did. We went to drive-in movies and had cookouts in our backyard. Most importantly, we sat down together as a family every night for dinner.

Donna flew the coop pretty early on, and Laurie was already gone. And then there was one. Laurie would drive into town to check in. Sometimes, she would make and eat dinner with me. During school breaks, I spent most of my time at their house.

I don't ever remember feeling lonely or scared. I was part of the new generation of latch-key kids. There were a few of us in the neighborhood that were home alone—maybe we should have formed a support group!

I do, however, remember the feeling of accomplishment after I did something that needed to be done. If a lightbulb blew, I'd grab the stepladder and change it. I cooked and cleaned for myself as well.

I remember one night, I walked into the kitchen, and there was water all over the floor in front of the refrigerator. I threw down a couple of towels and called the landlord. It was just a small hose that somehow became disconnected. He fixed it, cleaned up the water, told me to get a fan, and left. Till the day of her death, my mom never knew that happened. She didn't need to; I handled it.

I felt like a grown-up. Like I was able to control something, and I liked that feeling.

These self-taught skills, this independence, served me well—until it didn't. Turns out there is a very fine line between being self-sufficient and being a know-it-all control freak who doesn't need anything from anybody. As a child, they were my survival skills. As an adult, my nightmare.

You know what they say, "If you want something done right, you've got to do it yourself!" I *never* asked for help, I *never* sat down, I *never* relaxed. I was *way* beyond organized—more like anal-retentive. White-knuckling that control was also a form of protection. Nobody could let me down or disappoint me if I never gave them the chance to. I have left crushed egos and hurt feelings in my wake. Controlling everything, I rarely let my children help me make dinner, paint a bedroom, or repot a plant. Perhaps the most significant thing I remember is the day that my husband (at the time) and I had purchased some new framed prints for the living room. I was in the kitchen, cleaning the glass, and he was hammering the nails into the wall. When I walked back into the room, it was blatantly obvious that the nails weren't even. I said something so he could fix them. Instead, he handed me the hammer, and said, "You don't need me. You don't need me for anything. I feel like all I am is a paycheck." We both knew that what he said had nothing to do with the nails. That moment had been stirring and building within him for a very long time. Did it change anything? For a little while, it did. I searched deep inside for answers. The truth was, these ways, my ways, ran through every fiber of my being. It was how I survived as a child. How was I ever going to ask for help? How was I ever going to relinquish control? We eventually divorced, and other than losing thirty pounds, I didn't make any other changes as I started my next chapter. I had the attitude, "This is me, take it or leave it!"

My mom passed away when I was in my forties, at the age of seventy-three. A few weeks later, my father-in-law was diagnosed with cancer. There were other things going on as well, and I began thinking to myself, *My life is probably half-over already.* It all just made me realize how important it was to enjoy my next forty years; it was time to see a therapist. Of course, we eventually did a deep dive into my childhood. I learned so much; it was a wonderful experience for me. I wished so badly that I could have called my mom to tell her that everything was okay, and that I loved her.

Armed with the tools and resources I now had; I saw very slow but steady progress. I still did it all and still expected a lot out of people. I did, however, start doing some things for myself. This was a big deal. I had always put everyone's wants and needs before my own, then felt resentment when it wasn't reciprocated. It was twisted . . . who ever said it was my job to fulfill everybody's needs? Nobody! I took that on myself. I started walking, hiking, and even got into photography. I had *never* had hobbies. I didn't do anything for myself that created happiness—until then.

Five years ago, my husband, Matt, was taking me to New York City for my fiftieth birthday. In true form, everything was packed and ready to go, so I decided to go to the backyard to relax for a bit. I looked up to find a star-filled sky. I wondered where I fit within the vast universe that was looking back at me. I asked myself, *What do you have to show for the last fifty years, Kris? What is your legacy?*

Of course, I thought of the many blessings in my life, but I also thought of the wasted time, the stress that I caused myself (and others), selfishness, and regrets.

Just then, I stood up and created a huge sweeping motion from my head to my feet, and yelled, "CANCEL!"

I had no idea what it meant, but that's the word that spewed out of my mouth.

I immediately started creating a list of things that I had always wanted to accomplish. Mentors that I wanted to learn from and retreats that I wanted to attend. I wanted to grow.

It wasn't a bucket list. There was no trip to Greece, or a sports-car—this was different. It was my time to shine!

After my 2.0 revelation under the stars, there were so many things that I wanted to do. Start a business, become an author, improve my self-worth, but most importantly, learn to love myself. I knew that it was important to have a why—a *deep* why for each and every thing that I wanted to accomplish, but I had no idea how to create one. I began by researching "how to meditate" online. I read several self-help books, I started going to church again, I made my health a priority, I fell back on what I had learned in therapy, and I bought a beautiful pink gratitude journal and wrote down at least five things that I was grateful for every day.

They were the same dreams that I had *always* wanted to fulfill, only this time, I got out of my own way!

Every day, I felt stronger and more determined. Soon, my fear was in the rearview mirror.

Although I am still growing, still learning, and still struggling to relinquish control, I have never felt this level of peace or accomplishment. With age comes wisdom, and that is why it was so important for me to be part of this book. It is my hope to inspire, even just a few of you, with my story. Don't wait fifty years to leave your mark on the world like I did. Be flexible, not rigid, and go with the flow as best you can. Be aware of that fine line and make sure to keep it in check. And most importantly, believe in yourself.

Remember, the power is *within you* to create the life you want! To be unstoppable!

ABOUT KRISTINE N. MCQUOWN

Kristine is a best-selling author, speaker, and coach. She has written two children's books: the award-winning, *Good Boy, Nacho!* and *Super-Duper Seal of Approval* launching in 2023.

She founded studioknm, which embodies everything she loves: real estate investing, house flipping, photography, writing, and interior design. Kristine is also an author coach for a hybrid publishing company. She loves to share her knowledge by mentoring and coaching creative minds, specializing in personal branding, and organization.

Future endeavors include getting more children's books into the world and creating a nonprofit to assist families who need help getting their children into college. Currently, she is very excited to be writing a book alongside her husband about Generation X. It is a collection of 101 short stories written by Gen Xers, also launching in 2023.

Raised in New Hampshire and Michigan, Kristine now resides in Indiana with her husband, Matt, and their dog, Nacho. Together, they have four children and three grandchildren.

In her spare time, you will find her in the pool, traveling, volunteering, hiking, being inspired behind her camera, gardening, watching movies, cooking, eating pizza, and spending time with family and friends.

To connect with Kristine

www.studioknm.com	**Instagram:** @studioknm	
kris@studioknm.com	**Twitter:** @studioknm	
Facebook: studioknm	**LinkedIn:** studioknm	

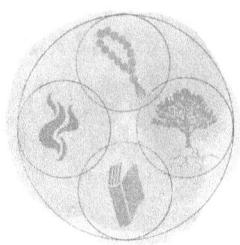

LETTER TO MY YOUNGER SELF

Shirah S. Penn, M.Ed.

OMG! Here I am, Gramma Shirah at eighty-four years young. Looking back over my life as little Shirsi, I wish I knew then what I know now. This is what I would have told myself.

Learn early on how to love yourself. What you say to yourself makes a difference. Of course, you want to please others, your parents, family, and friends, yet you don't have to be perfect. You will make mistakes and sometimes others will not be pleased with you. Only that's okay. Everyone makes mistakes. We are here to learn from them.

Learn early on what I later learned from Sid Simon: I am lovable and capable and so are you. You have the ability to be loving and lovable. You are capable of doing many things. Acknowledge yourself for the things you can do and be patient with yourself as you are learning new things. Sometimes we have to repeat things over and over again to learn them. Do not compare yourself to anyone else. We all learn things at different times. You might be better at sports than your friend, or they might learn to read before you. It doesn't matter. This isn't a race; it's a learning process. Unfortunately in school, you are given grades for how much you are learning. Sometimes your grade is just satisfactory, and that is okay. Acknowledge your achievements and accept your limitations. Trying to do somethings means you are putting forth the effort. It is okay to practice a skill. Sometimes when we do something over and over, we get better at that skill.

Dear younger self, my advice to you is to read Denise McCormick's book, *Never Mind the Monkey Mind.* Pay attention to the words you say when you talk to yourself. Learn early on to eliminate *don't, can't, should, shouldn't* from your vocabulary. Use words to encourage you to lift you up. You can do it! Go for your dreams. Create a great day! Set your intentions.

Even as young as you are, you can learn to take one hundred percent responsibility for your actions. If you make a mistake, say you're sorry and make amends. If you hurt someone's feelings, apologize and ask if you can make it better. Or better yet, look for ways to be kind and helpful. One of the ways to gain self-confidence is to actually do something out of your comfort zone. I was always afraid to sing in front of others. I didn't think I had a pretty enough voice. My fourth-grade teacher helped me by making it okay to sing in front of the class. The next time I wasn't so afraid. So my advice, dear younger self, is go for it anyway!

Another thing I would tell my younger self is love yourself and take care of yourself first. You don't need others to love and approve of you first. You must love and respect yourself. I think girls need to learn early on that they don't need a man's love to complete them. A lot of girls make mistakes in their teenage years because they think they need to be popular and pretty. Boys need to learn early on that doing work that they love will help them later on. The teenage years are full of confusing messages. Learning to figure this out will help in the future.

E + R = O as Jack Canfield teaches. Event + Response = Outcome. How you respond or react to an event will influence the outcome you get. Think of the consequences. Look for the lessons, child! Pay attention! Awareness is key. If you learn this lesson early on, you will know how to listen to the messages your heart is telling you.

You are learning so much from the moment you take your first breath. Learning how to pay attention to your breath is a tool you can learn. You learn early on that when you smile, it makes others feel good. When you cry as a baby, others think they have to fix you. You learn how to get attention by laughing or crying. As you get older, you can learn how to get attention by asking for what you want. A lot of times you hear grown-ups say, "Use your words." Ask for what you want.

Learn how to meditate as a young person. Your breath can help you calm down from strong emotions like anger, rage, frustration, fear. Learn to be in the present moment by focusing on your breath. Use the STAR method for relaxing: Stop, Take a deep breath, And Relax!

As you are learning to read and write, you can start keeping a journal. Drawing and writing about your feelings can help you focus on positive affirmations or messages. Some young people enjoy learning simple yoga positions. This helps create peace and harmony as you align your mind, body, and spirit. There are many wonderful programs for parents and teachers to help you as you learn more about life skills such as taking one hundred percent responsibility for your thoughts, feelings, and actions.

Last of all, little younger self, learn to be your own best friend. Treat yourself kindly as you would anyone else. You don't have to wait until you're sick and tired of being sick and tired to choose to be willing to love yourself and take good care of yourself.

After my retirement in 2002, I wanted to recreate myself as an entrepreneur. Much of my self-esteem came from my role as teacher, wife, and mother. I wanted to be a successful facilitator and author. So I ended up writing three children's books: *Gramma Shirah Says Words of Wisdom*, *More Words of Wisdom*, and *The Remarkable Journey*. I took many classes and workshops and attended networking groups to gain more confidence and self-esteem. My first book was all about quotes I shared with children. My second book was about quotes famous spiritual teachers taught me, and finally, my latest book is about how the colors of the rainbow influence our thoughts, feelings, and behavior.

Finally, dear younger self, forgive yourself for judging yourself. This is your journey. Make it a joyful one. You are in control of you!

ABOUT SHIRAH S. PENN, M.ED.

Shirah S. Penn is an eighty-four-year-young retired schoolteacher. She taught in Miami/Dade County for forty-two years from 1960 until 2002 when she retired. She taught K–3 and mostly taught in the first grade. As a teacher, Shirah received her master's degree in 1971. She was selected Peace Teacher of the Year by the Grace Contrino Abrams Peace Education Foundation for her work with Loving Circle Time. She was also chosen Teacher of the Year in 1994 by Palm Springs Elementary School.

So you can see that although Shirah received many testimonials for her teaching, she still felt she wasn't good enough. All her life, Shirah pursued studying the area of human psychology, particularly self-esteem. In 1971, after teaching in the classroom and being married for eleven years with two small children, Shirah received her master's degree in education from the University of Miami and got a divorce from what became an abusive relationship.

This began four years of group therapy under the direction of Dr. Arthur Stillman. She began reading many books such as *The Psychology of Self-Esteem* by Dr. Nathanial Brandon and *Transactional Analysis* by Erik Berne. She thought something was wrong with her that needed to be fixed. She knew instinctively that she couldn't blame her ex-husband for her low self-esteem. Shirah took a transformational seminar called Insight in 1981. One of her facilitators was Jack Canfield who later became her mentor and successful trainer of trainers. Shirah studied with Jack until 1994 and recently took some of his One Day to Success and Breakthrough to Success online and in-person trainings. Each time gave Shirah more tools to reinforce her desire to reach out to others, especially small children. Because of her journey, she is now ready to share what it has taken her so many years to learn: how to love herself.

This letter from Shirah to her younger self has all the lessons she learned on her journey. Hopefully you can gain some insights and possibly avoid her roadblocks. The limiting beliefs she wishes she had overcome as a young child are "I'm not good enough," "I'm not assertive or confident enough," and "Something is wrong with me." She knows you will learn your lessons on your journey in your own way. She hopes this is helpful. Many people have said to her, "I wish I had learned that when I was younger." The knowledge is here for you to gain when you choose to be willing to do what it takes to love yourself unconditionally and accept your shortcomings. No one is perfect.

To connect with Shirah

Shirahpenn@yahoo.com
Facebook: Shirah Penn

More titles from Shirah

Gramma Shirah Says Words of Wisdom
More Words of Wisdom
The Remarkable Journey

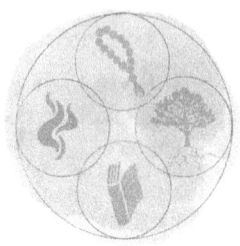

BREAKING BOUNDARIES

Michelle Picking

Have you ever stopped and started talking to yourself, not like in the sense of *Okay, I have this load of laundry to do next*, but as in *What the hell am I going to do now? Where do I go from here? How did I even get here? How do I break out of this place—the boundaries I've placed on myself or the ones placed on me by others?* Like you're tethered to something but have no idea how it happened.

In April 2014, I was bit by a dog at work. What I thought was a routine injury turned out to be the injury that turned my life upside down. So much so, that after five surgeries, resulting in losing tendons, ligaments, and some muscle mass, plus over a year of rehab, I was still told I may not have full use of my hand/wrist and the CRPS (chronic regional pain syndrome—fancy words for nerve pain and damage) would likely always be something I had to deal with.

This injury took me out of work and out of the gym (my happy place) but put me in a position to take care of my mother-in-law who was dealing with some health issues. I chose to walk away from my career and just focus on caring for her. However, losing her in October 2015, I once again found myself lost and had no direction; everything I'd done for over a year revolved around taking care of her, and now I had to find my way out again. So, I decided to start back at the gym again—a place I'd always loved. But dealing with the pain, lack of mobility from the injury, and my limitations also lead others to question why. *Why are you doing this? What's the point? Wouldn't it be easier to just continue the way you are?*

Would that have been the easier thing to do? Absolutely! But after thinking about why, I realized that I was tired of being leashed to things or thoughts that I wasn't choosing. I was tired of not being me. I was tired of looking in the mirror and not liking the person I saw there. I had been here once before in a previous abusive marriage, where I was told what to think, who to be, when to be places, and for how long. My friends were picked for me. I was told what to wear or not wear (legs too fat = "you can't wear shorts," oh, and I didn't for seven years). I didn't want to be that person anymore. I wanted and needed to figure out who I was and what I wanted to do with my life again. I wanted to break every rope, leash, and boundary that had been put on me that didn't enhance my life or thoughts.

I started back into the gym, the place that was usually a haven for me, but instead of being welcomed, I was made fun of, I was judged, all because I couldn't do a lot of the exercises or heavy weights. There were many days I'd be sitting in tears or coming home in tears, and people continued to ask *why, what's the point?* The point was I wasn't happy with who I was. I needed to stop allowing everyone else to dictate what I was capable of and who I wanted to be.

Sometimes it's so easy to just listen to all the voices who think they are allowed to dictate who you are, what box to put you in, what door to put you behind, or which rope to attach to you. But you must fight the voices and listen to the little one in your head, the one that cries out when your heart knows this isn't where or what you want it to be. The one that plucks at the rubber band to see how much it'll take before it breaks. The one whose voice gets louder the more you listen to it. The one who knows your heart.

My love of fitness had returned, but it wasn't enough. I needed a goal so I had something to really push for. So, I decided to take it a step further: I started to train for a Spartan race. The more pushback I got about why I was doing it or, even better, why I shouldn't be doing it—things like my age, my injury, all the what-ifs and "you shouldn't" or "can't"—just made me want to do it even more.

Training and running Spartan races with people I knew (and some I didn't) who challenged me was a catalyst for things to come. I'm not saying any of this was easy; it wasn't. But I had to start somewhere. During this time, I was also working toward getting a personal training certification so I could continue to find a way to help others become who they wanted to be. I had found one piece of the puzzle.

About a year or so into running Spartan races, I found another sport, Olympic Weightlifting. I stumbled into the sport by accident but completely fell head over heels for it. I stopped doing Spartan races and decided to focus solely on lifting. When I decided at the age of forty-eight in January of 2017, I was going to compete (yes, competition), oh, the comments I got. "You're going to get hurt." I already am, it can't get any worse. "But you could die." Not likely, but I could die driving my car to the grocery store, too, so there's that.

There are aspects of this sport that make it so incredibly tough, but those same aspects are what make it so great too. In this journey, I have found out so much about myself. My coach used to say to me "trust the process." For a long time I didn't fully understand what that meant. But I'm learning the longer I'm in the sport what it means.

For me, it's not just about the training, but about trusting in who you're becoming. This sport has taught me about patience. It's taught me about having more bad days than good ones and how to handle them, both the good and bad. It's not always easy, and I'm still a work in progress with it. The lesson isn't always an easy one, but you learn from the bad days, let go (or try to let go) of it, invite in what you want to focus on, and move into the next day. Whether the outcome is good or bad, your mindset has changed and how you handle all of it has changed as well. This sport has brought me into a space of checking in with myself to see where I am on any given day and knowing that whatever happens, I'll learn and grow from it. It's knowing that having a bad day is okay. It's knowing that I'll be back again tomorrow to do it all over again. It's knowing I'm stronger for learning to handle it. It's knowing *who* I am. I'm not saying I have it all mastered, I truly don't, but as with anything you choose to do and do well, it's a work in progress.

I still battle the doubters, the naysayers, the voices in my head, the ropes that try to sneak up and hold me back, but I've started to let my inner voice shout a lot louder, which results in my ability to shake off the chains and continue to move forward. I wish I would've been able to start competing earlier, but that wasn't the case, so I'm here now and doing everything I can. I wouldn't trade any part of the journey I've had in this sport for the world. As a matter of fact, I'd do it all over again.

In 2018, with my trainer certificate in hand, I decided to finally do something with the knowledge I'd gained and started to work for the YMCA. I loved working with clients and helping them push through their boundaries. Enter COVID; since I couldn't work outside the home any longer, we decided to build a gym at home. A place I could train, and I could also start training clients again when the time came. And Rise Up Fitness was born.

I believe in asking my clients to stretch and break through every door and tie they have as well. Not just from a fitness and nutrition aspect but on everything in their life. We set goals, we redefine definitions, and *they* choose where the boundaries are for themselves. Not what their doctor says, or their kids, or their parents or society has to say. We throw out the words *can't, won't, unable, I'm just,* and *I'm too.* These words are not allowed to be said in my gym.

Bottom line: I've set *my* boundaries. I've kicked in the door and walked through to the other side and become who I want to be not who I was told to be. I want that for each of you. If you feel like you've been put into a box, with no way out, let's stretch—no, break—the bands that are holding you back. You are *not* the disease or condition your doctor told you that you are. You're not *just* a mom. You're not too tall or too short or too anything! You're becoming the best version of the only you out there. Kick in the door and then run, don't walk through it. You *are* strong enough! You *are* brave enough! You don't fit the mold? Great! You shouldn't have to fit a mold to do what you love. What's the fun in that?

No one gets to decide who you are, what you do, or where your boundaries are except you. You do not have to live, work, or be in the confines of the boundaries someone else has put you in or "applied" to you. Whatever your passion is, find it, and BREAK EVERY BOUNDARY in order to do it.

ABOUT MICHELLE PICKING

Michelle is a certified personal trainer also holding certifications as a specialist in sports nutrition and strength and conditioning. She's also a USA Weightlifting Level 1 Coach, a USA weightlifting national referee, and currently holds all national records in the master's division W50–54, 64 kg category.

Michelle started Rise Up Fitness to continue her love of helping people and creating a safe, judgment-free space for them to train, grow, and find new boundaries they choose.

Michelle also decided to go back into her career as a veterinary technician/hospital manager and runs a veterinary surgical specialty practice. She uses her knowledge of how to grow to encourage her staff to continue their journey along the way as well.

Interested in working with Michelle and learning how to set your boundaries on your terms? Please reach out to her at the following places:

To connect with Michelle

boothmichelles@aol.com
910-670-2759
Facebook: Michelle Picking
Instagram: @michellepicking

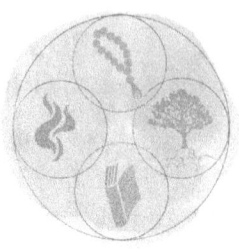

THAT GIRL

Elizabeth Gorn Stephenson

Wake up! WAKE UP! Your life is right now! Stop waiting to grow up, know what you want to do, or understand your direction. Just wake up and live NOW. Life is short and you need to stop wasting it!

So how are you going to do this? For me, I discovered what I call a three-pronged approach! First, take one hundred percent responsibility for your life. Stop being afraid everyone else knows more than you. Finally, step into the real authentic you, which will be the inner voice guiding you! In short, empower yourself!

Born into an entrepreneurial family, but subsequently reared by someone who doubted herself constantly, the messaging I received was pretty confusing. I believed in my heart I could do or be anything I wanted, and that was supported by those around me. Also supported by those around me were messages of "Who do you think you are?" and "Don't be cocky!" I took all those messages to heart because I wanted to be liked and loved. I've always known I had a spark . . . and indefinable "it" factor, if you will, but the conflicting messages made that hard to believe. I was in constant conflict with myself and as a result was waiting to grow up.

I got good grades in school. I was in theater, choir, etc. And in college, I was a busy girl, getting a degree in Communication Arts in the '80s, a time where that diploma and a buck could get you a cup of coffee! In short, what were my options with that degree?

In fact, it was such a useless degree, that I interviewed with a life insurance company . . . I think it was Northwestern Mutual? It was for a sales position. The rejection letter I received not only rejected me for that position, but also suggested I *never* work in sales! Obviously that was not confidence building, so, still not trusting myself, I drifted and bounced like a pebble in the river of life, accepting the first job I was offered out of college. I became an assistant manager trainee for a Walmart-like wannabe.

I got along with everyone except my direct boss, the manager. He was an incredible chauvinist. He felt I needed to take one of my days off to learn more and had me spend eight hours sorting and rearranging the women's intimate section. Then he had the gall to stop by every so often to ask me what I was learning. Such a rule follower and people pleaser, can you believe I actually made something up? What he needed was a good kick in the crot—shins! Just another example of how I didn't trust myself and was looking for the adultier adults to guide my journey.

Fast-forward a bit. I married my college sweetie who is five years older than me, who told me on our first date he was going to marry me! Ha! I asked how he knew that, and his answer was about as unromantic as it could get. He said, "There's nothing about you I can't stand." Really? Well, isn't that kind and generous of you? I was not impressed but I still said "I do." I can say thirty-eight years later, I get it, but that's for another chapter.

We settled into a college town where my husband was going to grad school. I'd been fascinated by advertising and it was a nice fit with my "valuable" degree, so here's where I finally began to take charge of my future. I wrote a very unconventional cover letter to an agency that wasn't currently looking to hire anyone, but because the letter was so odd, they wanted to meet the person who wrote it. It went something like "Dear X: I need your help. I'm addicted to *Advertising Age Magazine,* and I need a reason to read it." I got an interview and I wore a pale pink suit! And they hired me. I loved it, learned so much, and started to trust the spark.

One of the biggest lessons I learned while at the agency had to do with taking responsibility for fixing mistakes without pointing fingers or assigning blame. The goal was finding a solution to the problem. If it had to be reviewed later, it could be in a postmortem fashion so the same kind of mistake might be avoided in the future. It was never to put others in a difficult situation.

Now here's the funny part. Remember the insurance company that told me never to go into sales? Yeah, the agency put me into sales. After my initial wailing and gnashing of teeth, I was smitten . . . empowered by it! I'm told I'm a sales natural. I don't know about that, but I do know that I love people and helping them, so if that makes me a natural, so be it.

I was still waiting to feel like a grown-up. While I was growing, I still didn't trust myself, not completely. I knew I had potential, but I felt like there was some sort of brick wall in front of me that I needed to scale.

Life and a lot of stuff happened. We had two children. I changed jobs to manage the promotional products division of a different company—selling, of course.

Then I discovered *The Success Principles,* a book by Jack Canfield. The very first lesson in the book is about taking one hundred percent responsibility for your life. I understood the concept in a rudimentary way. You know, don't point fingers, but reading this principle is when my transformation really began.

When you take one hundred percent responsibility for your life, life opens up in a way that is completely liberating. When you are responsible, nobody can hold you back. When you are responsible, there is nobody to blame for problems. In fact, there are no longer problems, but challenges to face and overcome to build your confidence. It changes everything! Literally everything! You are no longer a victim of the whims of others, but instead are the victor of your own life!

Fear was fading. Trust in myself was blooming, and since I was now accepting responsibility for my own life, I was really in charge. The next lesson for me was more about empowerment, which ultimately leads to living authentically.

I'd been working with this other company for about six years, and the hubs thought maybe I should start my own competing business. His belief was that I could build a lifestyle in keeping with my values. OMGOSH! How could I possibly? What did I know about running a business? How could I be so mean to the company for whom I was working? The horror of it all!

Somehow, between his conviction that this was a good idea and me learning to leave fear behind and trust myself, I did it and never looked back. The final catalyst was the fact that I wanted a woman/family-friendly business. I wanted my employees to be loud and vocal about working *and* having a family. These were still the days when at work, you pretended you had no life outside of the office. I wanted Mom to feel free to go to Suzy's soccer match or Brian's band concert. I trusted that the work would get done. It worked. Talk about empowering all of us!

Also an eager learner and curious by nature, I was stifled where I had been. I knew I would never be more than a valued employee kept on a need-to-know level. With my own business, I got to know everything, and it suited me well. I was forced to make my own empowered decisions. After all, who was I going to ask?

My husband was the one who first empowered me. Empowerment can come to you from others. It can be the engine starter. Do I wish I'd initially empowered myself? Yes, but there have been plenty of times since to empower myself. It's nice to have someone believe in you so much to help get the motor running!

During my thirty years as a business owner, selling promotional products, I have learned to trust myself a whole lot more. I've also learned more about my strengths and weaknesses. And I worked hard to take one hundred percent responsibility for everything that came my way. I was empowered, but I still didn't feel like I'd scaled the wall of what I now knew was authenticity! I was starting to think about legacies, etc. I knew I felt strongly about empowering others to take charge of their lives, and I was beginning to realize that authenticity was a critical piece of that along with the accepting of responsibility.

Through a winding path that took me to the depths of self-doubt, I finally became the chief Dreamweaver of The Empowered Women's Experience. Initially it was the Entrepreneurial Women's Expo, a daylong event with speakers, workshops, and networking. I bought it from the woman who created it. It was a great event, but it was a very hard lesson for me as our personalities didn't mesh at all.

I kept hoping she would let me know what I didn't know, but instead she filled my life with "oh shit" moments. "Why haven't you done this or that?" And I fell into old habits playing the blame game. It was her fault it wasn't going well. I fell deep into the well until I held my first event. She attended and cornered me asking me about all these things she thought I was doing wrong. I was a hot mess. Then I stood up straighter. I took a deep breath and told her that I was in charge and in the middle of running the event my way. I got my "groove back," took responsibility, and did my first solo as *authentically me*!

What started as a business is really a passion project. Being an entrepreneurial event was too limiting. Women who didn't own businesses felt it wasn't for them. In my mind, there isn't a woman alive who isn't an entrepreneur. Even if she doesn't own a business, she is juggling many businesses. She's usually the glue that keeps things all together. So, I made it more inclusive by focusing on empowerment to fulfill my passion of helping other women *wake up*.

I believe women are the biggest impediment to their own empowerment and authenticity. We worry what others will think of us. We feel like imposters. We reject the concept of faking it until we make it, although that's what men have been taught to do since the beginning of time. We don't want to hurt anyone's feelings, and yet we hurt our own. Look at me. I'm a grown woman and am only now finding my total confidence, authenticity, and empowerment. So how do we fight this? Again, we take one hundred percent responsibility for our own lives.

At a grass roots level, when you take one hundred percent responsibility for the direction of your life, you can ignore those exterior forces. They no longer matter. I believe we doubt ourselves so much that we stand in the shadows, looking for someone to tell us our value and show us we are capable. Yet when we rely on others, we're getting the information from their frame of reference. Do they really know who we are? If we really think about it, do they even care? They're busy trying to sort it out in their own lives.

It's also time to decide that you are the adultier adult at least in terms of your own life. Be. Do. React. Escort fear out of the room! There's always a way to pivot so there is nothing to fear! *Believe* in yourself and *live*. Try something that appeals to you . . . anything. And if it doesn't work out, shout "NEXT!" and move on. And *be authentically* you. It's really the best guidance system you'll ever have. You feel the right decision in your gut when you listen for it! It is so liberating.

I've discovered that being authentic is *fun*! I love exploring the quirky me and finding those who are attracted to it. Some don't get me. Some don't like me. But it's okay because through authenticity, I have discovered my pack . . . some of those soul sisters! I have become "THAT GIRL!"

With the Empowered Women's Experience, I'm trying to teach women to be "THAT GIRL." THAT GIRL is the one who lives life as a grand adventure. She is always moving toward something. She is passionate about learning . . . about herself, the world, others. She may reach her goals or maybe she won't, but she knows it's about the journey and being who she is. That's authenticity, and it can be scary.

I've always been a bit of an odd duck. I think that comes with the spark. It just is what it is, but it took a kick in the gut to get me to really embrace my authenticity. Last year I was diagnosed with lung cancer, having never smoked a day in my life. I went through surgery, chemo, and radiation. Currently, I have no detectable disease so we can move along. Nothing to see here.

However, up until then, cancer had always been my biggest fear. once you've faced your biggest fear, what is there to fear? Cancer reminded me that I want to be fearless. It reminded me that life is short.

Now, I'm focusing on what I like to do and what I want to do while building some sort of legacy. What is fear, after all, but false evidence appearing real and keeping you stuck in the same rut. Fear is a waste of time. I'm afraid of skydiving and don't plan to do it, but if there's something I want to do, I'm doing it . . . and doing it now! Write a chapter in a book? Why not?!

I was also reminded how much I want to be who I really am. I've found that authenticity leads to deeper relationships, more understanding, and more richness in life. Life is too short to be who others want you to be. There's only time to be YOU. I desperately want the same for other women around me.

Don't waste another minute waiting to grow up. Meet yourself where you are, embracing every imperfection because it makes you unique. Don't waste another minute on fear. Fear about anything but true danger is just an illusion. Don't waste another minute trying to be who you think you should be instead of being authentically you! Your soul only soars when you love it and live its purpose. You are beautifully, perfectly you! You are THAT GIRL!

ABOUT ELIZABETH GORN STEPHENSON

Elizabeth Gorn Stephenson comes from an entrepreneurial family and has had her own promotional products business, Custom Stuff, for thirty years. Additionally, she is passionate about helping women believe in themselves! As the owner and CEO of The Empowered Women's Experience and home of THAT GIRL, she forges a safe community for women to explore who they are and who they want to become through networking, workshops, and events. Watch for Elizabeth's new podcast this spring, *THAT GIRL CONFIDENTIAL—Tell all tales of self-discovery and self-empowerment,* where featured guests will share how they went from the shadows into the sun! Married for thirty-eights years to a fabulous and supportive husband and mom to two grown kids who are equally supportive, Elizabeth is also a rescue cat mom and shares more pictures of them than her humans! She loves learning, reading, photography, travel, pop music (not rap!), paper quilling, watching waves, *The Marvelous Mrs. Maisel* and most recently is addicted to mahjong and canasta! And if conditions are forgiving, she can also swear like a sailor!

To connect with Elizabeth

EWESC.com
success@ewesc.com

Have you ever dreamed of
becoming a published author?
Do you have a story to share?
Would the world benefit
from hearing your message?

Then we want to connect with you!

The *Inspired Impact Book Series* is looking to connect with
women who desire to share their stories with the goal of
inspiring others.

We want to hear your story!

Visit www.katebutlerbooks.com to learn more
about becoming a Featured Author in the #1 International
Best-selling *Inspired Impact Book Series*.

Everyone has a story to share!
Is it your time to create your legacy?

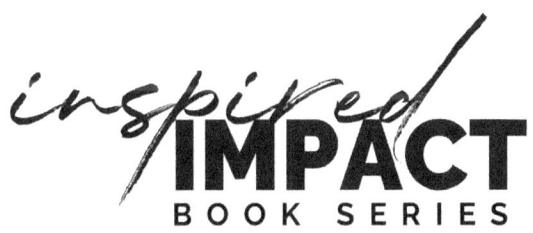

May the words of these pages inspire you to continue to come back home to yourself, remember who you are and ignite your infinite light to shine bright in this world! We love you. Thank you for taking this journey with us.

Authors of Dear Younger Self

REPRINTED WITH PERMISSIONS